THE SILVER SHADOW

THE SILVER SHADOW
AND
OTHER DAY DREAMS

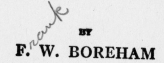

BY

F. W. BOREHAM

AUTHOR OF

'THE OTHER SIDE OF THE HILL,' 'FACES IN THE FIRE,' 'MUSHROOMS ON THE MOOR,' 'THE GOLDEN MILESTONE,' 'MOUNTAINS IN THE MIST,' 'THE LUGGAGE OF LIFE,' ETC., ETC.

THE ABINGDON PRESS

NEW YORK CINCINNATI

First Edition Printed November, 1918
Reprinted April and December, 1919; May, 1920

CONTENTS

PART I

PART II

PART III

BY WAY OF INTRODUCTION

THESE are only some random reflections. The reflection of a thing is not the thing itself; but then again, you would sometimes miss the thing itself but for the reflection of the thing. Years ago, in the interior of New Zealand, I was strolling along the green banks of a lovely lake that nestles serenely among the huge snow-capped mountains. Suddenly, on a projecting ledge of rock, almost hidden by the dense forestry, I came upon a little Maori maiden. She was lying at full length, face downwards, peering into the placid sheet of water. Her own comely countenance, the waving grasses that almost buried her, the green boughs and bright blossoms overhead, and the bird that was calling from the branches, were all most exquisitely mirrored in those tranquil and crystalline depths. It had probably never occurred to her to admire, as she looked *about* her and *above* her, the rich foliage of the rata, the tossing plumes of pampas, the sword-like blades of flax, and the shining plumage of the tui. But the *reflections* in the water fascinated her. 'Look!' she cried excitedly, in her expressive and musical native speech, 'it is *a sea of silver shadows*!' That is precisely what I should like this book to be.

FRANK W. BOREHAM.

ARMADALE, MELBOURNE, AUSTRALIA,

PART I

I

DOMINOES

'What do you say to a game of dominoes?'

I was never more surprised. He was the last man from whom I should have expected such a suggestion. But that is the best of living in this world. On the other planets things happen according to rote; you can see with half an eye what is coming next. But this world is a box of tricks, a packet of surprises. You never know one minute what the next minute holds in store. Everything is effervescent, full ot snap and sparkle.

'What do you say to a game of dominoes?'

No sooner said than done. The little wooden box appeared from a cupboard in the corner. The black and white tablets were emptied with a clatter on to the table, turned face downwards, and divided between us. We arranged and examined them, and got to business. It is a very old game, and had a great vogue a couple of centuries ago. The sport consists, as everybody knows, in always matching your companion's piece. You must follow his suit, or you lose your turn. If he plays a six, you must lay a six beside it. If he plays a four, you must match it with a four. If you cannot respond to the challenge of his piece, you hold your hand and he plays again. But to miss your turn is to submit to a heavy handicap, for the player who first gets rid of all his dominoes wins the game.

And so we played at dominoes, following that first game with a second and a third. It occurred to me whilst we were playing that life itself is but a game of dominoes. Its highest art lies in matching your companion's pieces. Is he glad? It is a great thing to be able to rejoice with those who do rejoice. Is he sad? It is a great thing to be able to weep with those that weep. It means, of course, that if you answer the challenge every time, your pieces will soon be gone. But, as against that, it is worth remembering that victory lies not in accumulation, but in exhaustion. The player who is first left with empty hands wins everything.

I have already confessed that when my host made his abrupt suggestion last night, I was never more surprised in my life. He was the last man whom I should have suspected of a fondness for dominoes. If he had said billiards or bagatelle or draughts or chess, I should not have wondered in the least. But dominoes! I could scarcely imagine him playing dominoes! That is the pity of it. You never know how many people there are who are waiting for a chance of playing dominoes with you. The most unlikely people play at dominoes. Mr. O. Henry, in one of his short stories, tells of a remarkable interview between a burglar and his prey. The unhappy victim was in bed.

'Hold up both your hands!' commanded the burglar, pointing his revolver at the head on the pillows. The man in bed raised his right hand.

'Up with the other one!' ordered the burglar. 'You might be amphibious and shoot with your left! Hurry up!'

'Can't raise the other one,' pleaded the victim.

'What's the matter with it?'

'Rheumatism in the shoulder!'

The burglar stood for a moment or two in deepest contemplation.

'It's good for you,' he observed at length, 'that rheumatism and me happens to be old pals. I got it in my left arm, too!'

And then the pair proceeded to discuss the nature of their aches and pains; they debated symptoms, premonitions, and the effect of a change of the weather. Then they compared notes as to the respective merits of opodeldoc, witch-hazel, essence of evergreen, rattlesnake oil, Chiselum's Pills,

Finkleham's Extract, Omberry's Ointment, Pott's Pain Pulverizer, Blickerstaff's Blood Builder, and a number of similar preparations. By the time they had exhausted the list they were the best of friends, and the burglar sympathetically helped his victim into his clothes.

You would never have suspected that the burglar was eager for a game of dominoes. But as soon as his victim explained that he suffered from rheumatism in the left shoulder, the burglar matched the experience with an identical one of his own, and from that moment the game proceeded merrily enough. The most unlikely people play at dominoes.

Or, if it be objected that Mr. Henry's story is merely a frolic of a vivacious and versatile imagination, let us turn from fiction to fact. From Mr. Henry's pleasant fantasies to the sombre biography of a Lord Chief Justice is a far flight. I am very fond, however, of Barry O'Brien's great *Life of Lord Russell of Killowen*. And few things in the book are more striking than the biographer's story of the way in which his friendship with Lord Russell—then Mr. Charles Russell—began. 'In the summer of 1875,' Mr. O'Brien says, 'my father died, and, in the winter of the same year, poor MacMahon passed away. Within a few months I lost my two best friends in the world. It was a great blow and a great sorrow to me. One evening about six o'clock I went into the "Cock" to dine. I felt very miserable, and, I dare say, I looked it. I had just commenced my chop when in walked Charles Russell. I think there was not a man in London whom I liked less to see at that moment. I shrank from what I conceived to be his cold, hard, unsympathetic nature.' O'Brien tried to gulp his chop hurriedly in order to get away from his frigid acquaintance. But Russell came and sat at the same table right opposite him. 'He started the conversation. He spoke about MacMahon with a sympathy and a feeling which I did not in the least expect. Indeed, I never, I think, saw so complete a metamorphosis in any man as I saw in Russell that evening. It seemed to me that, while we talked, the whole character of his face changed. The hard, masterful look was gone. The disagreeable combative expression of the mouth had vanished. The eyes were soft and kind. The voice was subdued and low; and now and then a charming smile would play over his features, lighting up what was truly a noble countenance.' And thus began a friendship which lasted and deepened through many years. Now here was a surprise! It never occurred to O'Brien that Charles Russell could respond to his friend's sorrow with a sorrow of his own. He never suspected him of sympathy. But O'Brien learned that day, as I learned last night, and as we all learn sooner or later, that the most unlikely people play at dominoes.

For the beauty of dominoes is that any one can play the game. You have but to grasp two essential principles. You must clearly understand in the first place that, at every turn, you must match your companion's play, laying a six beside his six, a three beside his three, and so on. And you must clearly understand in the second place that the whole secret of success lies, not in hoarding, but in spending. Victory lies in paying out the little ivory tablets with as prodigal a hand as possible. It is better in dominoes to give than to keep. It is better to play a domino with twelve black dots on it than a domino with only two. Dominoes teaches me to 'measure my life by loss instead of gain, not by the wine drunk, but by the wine poured out.' Anybody who can firmly grasp these two fundamental principles may become an expert and brilliant domino player.

One of the most accomplished players that I have ever met was introduced to me by Mrs. Florence Barclay. I refer, of course, to Mrs. O'Mara, the nurse, in *The Mistress of Shenstone*. Lady Inglesby had received news that her husband had been killed on active service at Targai, and she was being attended by Doctor Sir Deryck Brand. Turning suddenly to the nurse, Sir Deryck caught a strange look of dumb anguish in those quiet eyes.

'Mrs. O'Mara,' he said, with a hand upon her shoulder, 'you have sorrow of your own!'

She drew away in terror. 'Oh, hush!' she whispered. 'Don't ask! Don't unnerve me, sir! Help me to think of her only!' Then, more calmly, 'Only, only, sir, as you are so kind'—she drew from her pocket a crumpled telegram and handed it to the doctor—'Mine came at the same time as hers!' she said simply.

The doctor unfolded the War Office message.

'*Regret to report Sergeant O'Mara killed in assault on Targai yesterday.*'

'He was a good husband,' said the nurse, 'and we were very happy.'

The doctor held out his hand. 'I am proud to have met you, Mrs. O'Mara,' he said. 'This seems to me the bravest thing I have ever known a woman do!'

She smiled through her tears. 'Thank God, sir,' she said tremulously, 'but it is easier to bear my own sorrow when I have work to do for her.'

What does it mean? It means that Mrs. O'Mara had thoroughly mastered the two essential principles of dominoes. She had learned to lay her own experience of anguish beside the experience of Lady Inglesby; and she had learned that the secret of life lay, not in saving her heart's best treasure, but in spending it. She might have worried; but she worked.

She reminds me of Charles Lamb. Charles Lamb knew how to play dominoes. How, at every turn, he matched his sister's moods, laughing with her when she was in the humour to laugh, and weeping with her when she wept! It is a dramatic and tender story, the story of Lamb's compassionate ministry to his afflicted sister. Charles had himself known the horrors of insanity, and, after his recovery, he watched over poor Mary with a brooding and vigilant solicitude. He simply lived for her, and tended her until his death with a most affecting and beautiful constancy. 'Whenever,' says one who knew them well, 'whenever an approach of one of her fits of insanity was announced by some irritability or change of manner, Charles would take Mary under his arm and set out for the asylum. It was very affecting to encounter the young brother and sister walking together across the fields, bathed in tears, bent on this painful errand. They used to carry a strait-waistcoat between them.' Charles and Mary Lamb were playing dominoes, that was all. Against each experience of hers, he set a similar experience of his own. The charm of dominoes is that it always calls out your best. As I have said, it is better to lay down a tablet with twelve dots than a tablet with only two. The more I give, the richer I am. Lady Inglesby's grief appealed to all that was best in Mrs. O'Mara, and, matching heart-break with heart-break, she gave herself without stint. Mary Lamb's affliction appealed to all that was best in the gentle Elia, and, matching suffering with suffering, he gave himself without stint to his brotherly ministry. And both Mrs. O'Mara and Charles Lamb were brought nearer to success in life's great game through squandering the soul's treasure with such a lavish hand.

And what about Paul? Was not Paul a past-master at both the principles that govern a game of dominoes? He knew that the secret of success was not to save your pieces, but to get rid of them. 'Most gladly, therefore,' says he, 'will I spend and be spent for you.' And was there ever one as clever at matching his companion's play? 'I made myself a slave,' he says, 'that I might win the slaves; unto the Jews I became as a Jew, that I might gain the Jews; to them that are under the law, as under the law, that I might gain them that are under the law; to them that are without law, I became as without law, that I might gain them that are without law. To the weak became I as weak, that I might gain the weak; I am made all things to all men, that I might by any means save some.' That was the greatest game of dominoes ever played!

And surely this is the secret of the wonderful appeal that the Cross makes to me. It is divine sorrow exactly matching human sorrow. 'Humanity,' as one of the greatest of our lawyers put it, 'has been deeply wounded somewhere.' So 'He was wounded for our transgressions; He was bruised for our iniquities.' He was crucified between two thieves as an emblem of the fact that He laid His anguish beside our human anguish, His heartache and heart-break beside our own. In matching our sorrows He poured out His own divinest treasure without stint and without reserve. He gave everything; and, because He gave everything, He must win everything. Yes, He must win everything! The appeal of the Cross carries all before it. The 'Lady of the Decoration' tells how, one Christmas-time, she gave a magic-lantern entertainment to the mothers of the Japanese children who attended the kindergarten. The little Japanese women, who had never seen a piano before, much less a magic-lantern, came in force. But they were unimpressed. 'I showed them a hundred slides. I explained until I was hoarse. I gesticulated and orated to no purpose. They remained silent and stolid. By-and-by there was a stir, heads were raised and necks craned. A sudden interest swept over the room. I followed their gaze, and saw on the sheet the picture of Christ toiling up the mountain under the burden of the cross. The story was new and strange to them, but the fact was as old as life itself. At last they had found something that touched their own lives and brought the quick tears of sympathy to their eyes.' They felt that here was One who had suffered just as they had suffered, One who felt exactly as they felt, One whose deep and terrible experience exactly answered to their own. He was the very Saviour they needed; the match was perfect!

> How sweet the fitness betwixt Him and me!
> My sin needs grace like this, so rich and free;
> And weakness, helpless weakness, such as mine,
> Is needed to make perfect strength divine.

These Japanese mothers felt that the story that they heard that night fitted their lives as glove fits hand, as key fits lock, as domino fits domino. When the great wide world makes the same luminous discovery, then, depend upon it, the conflict of the ages is over and the Christ has won!

II

THE THRUSHES ON THE LAWN

I AM writing on the lawn—in more senses than one. A lawn is a lovable, lazy, luxurious place. The thrushes and I think that there is no place like it. You never hurry on a lawn—except in play. You never see a clock on a lawn. Clocks were only invented after man's exclusion from Paradise, and are a badge of his fallen condition. The lawn is too much like Paradise to tolerate a clock. The clock, as Tennyson says in *In Memoriam,*

> . . . the clock
> Beats out the little lives of men.

On the lawn you escape from such a murderous castigation. There may, it is true, be a sundial on the lawn; but between a clock and a sundial there is all the difference in the world. A clock is a horrible thing; it is vulgar, loud, self-assertive; it stares you out of countenance; it keeps on talking, and, once an hour at least, positively screams. But a sundial is modest. If you wish to see its face, you must go right up to it and do the staring yourself. It is silent; it never ticks, or chimes, or strikes, or even cries 'Cuckoo.' Like the good little children of whom we once heard, it only speaks when it is spoken to; it is seen, but not heard. Like those same model children, it goes to sleep at sunset. You spend an evening by the fireside, and the clock on the mantelpiece glares at you in the most shameful fashion, and says the rudest things. But the dial on the lawn hides its face so bashfully, and holds its tongue so carefully, that you might sit there for hours totally unconscious of its presence. The sundial is the soul of courtesy; it never hints that it is time to go. It has lived on the lawn so long that it has caught the spirit of the place.

The lawn loves the lounger; it loathes the hustler. You never get flurried on the lawn. You saunter, stroll, and loll about, unhurried and unworried. If the fancy takes you to sit, you sit as you would never dream of sitting anywhere else. You squat or lounge in some entirely unconventional posture, a posture that is sanctioned only by the etiquette—the easy-going etiquette—of the lawn. Or, desiring neither to stand nor sit, you sprawl; and as you sprawl, the lawn receives you with a gentle caress and takes you to its heart. The lawn was made for lolling and loitering and lounging and sprawling; and it only admits you to its confidence when you abandon yourself to its moods without reserve. Some day I shall address an ode to the lawn; the rhyming is so obvious. Nobody could write ten lines on such a theme without making 'lawn' to rhyme with 'yawn.' Lawns and yawns go together.

As I sit scribbling here on this Australian lawn, I am thinking of the thrushes on a lovely lawn far, far away. I am afraid, now that I come to think of it, that the thrushes that I knew must have sung their last song and taken their long, long flight; for it is years and years since I last visited the place. All the oceans of the world now roll between that lawn and me. When I was quite a little chap I used to leave home for school about half an hour before my father set out for his office. I rebelled every morning against this obvious inequity. But I never allowed the sun to go down upon my wrath, for, in the afternoon, I reached home some hours before my father, and I felt that I had the better of him. But it happened that my father had as a client a very old lady who lived about half-way between the home and the school.

'Frank,' my father would sometimes say, 'I am going to start early this morning. I have to call on Mrs. Faulkner. Do you care to come?'

He knew that, to me, a visit to Mrs. Faulkner was the summit of mortal bliss. Mrs. Faulkner was a lovely old lady, with a dainty cap and snowy ringlets, who seemed to be quite lost in the cushioned recesses of an enormous arm-chair. In a little cupboard within her reach she kept an amazing variety of biscuits, cakes, chocolates, nuts, sweetmeats, sugar-plums, almonds and raisins, and other things in which small boys take particular interest. The carpet was so soft that my feet seemed to sink right into it; the furniture was massive and antique; whilst a wonderful company of old gentlemen with powdered hair and old ladies with crinkled ruffs looked down at me from the oil-paintings round the walls. In winter-time Mrs. Faulkner was always seated beside a fire that seemed ten times as large as any other fire that I had ever seen; but it was not in winter-time that I liked to visit Mrs. Faulkner best. On summer mornings the great French windows at the far end of the room stood wide open, and you could step straight out on to the lawn. And such a lawn! It was as level as a billiard-table; a spirit-level would have discovered no flaw. All round it there were wallflowers and sweet-williams, carnations and mignonette, sweet-peas and nasturtiums, lavender and musk. Mrs. Faulkner could sit enthroned in her enormous chair, sipping her port wine and reading *The Times,* and could inhale the full, rich fragrance of the flowers. The breath of the lawn seemed to fill the room; whilst the humming of the bees made you raise your voice to secure a hearing.

As soon as my father opened his bag, took out his papers, and settled down to business, I used to edge away towards the great windows that stood open to the lawn. I liked to stand there for awhile watching the giddy dance across the green of the pretty butterflies. The air seemed a-flutter with their white wings, whilst sometimes my uncontrollable excitement compelled me to interrupt the serious conversation of my seniors in order to draw attention to a real live Tortoise-shell or a splendid Purple Emperor that had just settled on one of the rose-trees. And then there were the thrushes! There were always half a dozen fine olive-brown thrushes hunting for grubs on the lawn, and I could hear others singing in the apple-trees down the garden. Perhaps those distant choristers had finished their breakfast on the lawn, or perhaps they were singing at the very thought of it. Anyhow, these on the lawn captivated me; they were so pert and impudent and unafraid. I used to fancy that they knew Mrs. Faulkner, and therefore felt no fear. They would look cheekily up at me, displaying to advantage their pretty mottled breasts, when I appeared in the open window-way. They would come on, hopping twenty steps without a pause, quite unabashed by my presence. The fact that my father could, on ordinary mornings, remain at home half an hour after I had left, paled into insignificance. Here, surely, was the life luxurious! I tried to imagine what it must feel like to be a thrush or a butterfly on Mrs. Faulkner's lawn! But my imagination failed me at every attempt!

The lawn, I say, is a leisurely place. I do not mean merely that it coaxes me to restfulness; that is a *consequence.* I mean that it is itself leisurely; that is a *cause.* I lounge and loiter on the lawn because I have caught the contagion of its own repose. You cannot bustle on a lawn if you try. You cannot lay a lawn as you lay a carpet. You cannot hurry a lawn as you hurry a plant in a conservatory. You must wait the lawn's time, and the lawn's time is a long time. I began by saying that, beneath these blue Australian skies, I am writing on the lawn. But an expert in the matter of lawns would pooh-pooh the idea of lawns in Australia. I heard recently of a party of young Australians who, in the course of a visit to the Homeland, found themselves moving amidst the classic shades of Oxford. Presently one of them was impressed by the beauty of the lawns. Oh, those lawns of England! Harold Begbie knew what he was talking about when, in his ballad of 'Britons Beyond the Seas,' he pictures the colonist as thinking fondly and wistfully of the lawns he left behind him:

And it's, O for a glimpse of England and the buds that her
    garden yields,

The delicate scent where her hedges wind and the shimmering green of her fields,
The roll of her downs, and the lull of her streams, and the grace of her dew-drenched lawns,
And the calm of her shores where the waters wash rose-tinged with her thousand dawns!

'*The grace of her dew-drenched lawns!*' It always rushes to memory when we, in these new lands, think tenderly of the treasures we left in the old one. But I digress. I left my party of young Australians admiring the velvety lawns of Oxford. 'I say,' exclaimed one of them, addressing himself to the caretaker, 'I say, how do you manage to get your lawns like this?' and he pointed admiringly to the sheen of greensward at his feet. 'Oh,' replied the old man, 'that's easy enough! You just mows it, and then you rolls it, and then you waters it; and then you mows it again, and rolls it again, and waters it again; and you goes on like that *for a few hundred years,* and you gets a lawn like *that!*' and he too pointed fondly to the green that he loved. 'You just goes on like that *for a few hundred years!*' Yes, a lawn is a leisurely place. You cannot lay a lawn as you lay a linoleum. When I lounge upon the lawn I am drinking in its own delicious patience and repose.

Everything about the lawn is restful; the very colour of the lawn is restful. What a dreadful place the lawn would be if it were any colour but green!

A field of bluebells charms you; a field of poppies fascinates you; a field of buttercups dazzles you; but we should not like the lawn to be blue or scarlet or gold. The eyes would tire and ache; we should go indoors to rest them; it is only the green that soothes and satisfies. I know a banker who always uses a sheet of green blotting-paper for this very reason.

I have been reading Dr. C. W. Valentine's *Psychology of Beauty.* In his chapter on 'The Beauty of Colour' he speaks of some remarkable experiments made by Mr. W. H. Winch. Mr. Winch tested two thousand London school-children, and then a number of adults, as to their favourite colours. The results were most interesting, and may be briefly summarized. With the tiny tots, red was an easy first, and green was nowhere! With the intermediates, blue was first, and green had improved its position. With the senior scholars, blue was still first, but green had risen to second place. With grown men, green was first, and blue had fallen to the second position. Now why this growing popularity of green as life wears on? Mr. Valentine thinks that it is because green is the restful colour. The tiny children know no rapture but the ecstasy of movement; sitting still is torture unendurable; bedtime is greeted with sulks and tears; they have no love for green. But as life goes on, rest becomes less distasteful; then positively attractive; until, little by little, green comes into its own. When Mrs. Alexander sang of 'A Green Hill Far Away' she displayed a flash of real psychological and spiritual insight. Calvary allures the weary. Tired hearts love the lawn.

The lawn is a means of grace. It makes me stroll and saunter, lounge and sprawl; and all this is good for me. Half the art of life consists in rightly adjusting labour to repose. I may lose my soul, it is true, through being too much on the lawn; laziness is lifelessness. But the lawn sets no premium on laziness. For listen, what is that? Whir-r-r-r! It is my neighbour on the other side of the hedge hard at work with his lawn-mower. 'Whir-r-r-r!' cries the lawn-mower; and it is the lawn-mower's way of saying that if you want leisure, you must work; if you want to lounge, you must labour! Oh, the wisdom of this lawn of mine! It knows that I may lose my soul through being too much on the lawn; laziness is lifelessness. So it makes me labour. But it knows, too, that I may lose my soul through never visiting the lawn; perpetual motion is a fool's paradise. So it makes me lounge. Here on the lawn I regain the poise of my spirit, the equilibrium of my soul. I learn to be leisurely. I hear no more the ticking and the screaming of the clock.

John Ruskin lived in the Lake Country, and dearly loved a lawn. And Ruskin learned the lessons that the lawn can so well teach. The graces that most impressed him were its humility and its cheerfulness. 'Its *humility,* in that it seems created only for lowest service, appointed to be trodden on. Its *cheerfulness,* in that it seems to exult under all kinds of violence and suffering. You roll it, and it is the stronger the next day; you mow it, and it multiplies its shoots, as if it were grateful; you tread upon it, and it only sends up richer perfume. Spring comes, and it rejoices with all the earth, glowing with variegated flame of flowers, waving in soft depth of fruitful strength. Winter comes, and, though it will not mock its fellow plants by growing then, it will not pine and mourn, and turn colourless or leafless as they. It is always green, and is only the brighter and gayer for the hoar-frost.' Peace, lowliness, cheerfulness; who would not visit the lawn when such fair, fragrant blossoms are flourishing around its borders?

I am surprised that, with so much to be learned from the lawn, there is nothing about it in the Bible. So far as I can see, the word never occurs. And yet, and yet—what is this? In that greatest of all the Messianic Psalms—the seventy-second—I read that, when the long-looked-for Saviour at last appears, *'He shall come down like rain upon the mown grass.'* And the best comment is that of Michael Fairless in *The Roadmender.* 'The evening sky,' she says, 'was clouding fast; the sound of rain was in the air. As I lingered at the gate, drinking in the scent of the field and the cool of the coming rain, the first drops fell on my upturned face and kissed the grasses at my feet, and I was glad. David, child of the fields and the sheepfolds, his kingship laid aside, sees through the parted curtain of the years the advent of his greater Son, and cries his last prophetic prayer: *He shall come down like rain on the mown grass!* In great pity comes the rain; gentle, refreshing, penetrating; and the grass is comforted by its tender touch and cool caress. Even so *He* came and still shall come.'

Like rain on the mown grass—even so He came!

Like rain on the mown grass—even so He still shall come whenever and wherever bruised and lacerated souls look up, like the mown grass, for His healing and refreshing grace.

III

GYP

GYP was a fox-terrier. Although no dog-fancier would have looked a second time at him, his portrait, finely framed, hangs over the study mantelpiece. A photograph of his grave in the garden may be seen in the corner of the dining-room. John Broadbanks often tells his brother ministers that Gyp was the means of his conversion. Some of them know the story, having, in a moment of fraternal confidence, heard him tell it. It is worth recording.

The pretty old manse at Silverstream is a model in its way. As a badge of its nationality, two tall New Zealand palms stand, like giant sentries, right in front of the house. But, to show that tender thoughts of older lands hang pleasantly about the place, a pair of laburnums guard the gate and drape it towards Christmas-time with their graceful tassels of gold. Roses monopolize the front border, and are evidently tended by a hand that loves them. A row of apple-trees holds possession of the garden along one side of the manse, whilst, away to the other, there stretches a trim and sunny lawn. The blackbirds can never make up their minds whether it is better fun singing in the apple-trees on the eastern side of the manse or hopping about the soft green lawn on the west. The manse itself is a dreamy old place, with cosy rooms, a long hall, an immense kitchen, and spacious sun-bathed verandahs. You hear nothing in the daytime but the songs of the birds in the tall blue-gums near by, and at night the stillness is only broken by the chirping of a cricket.

I do not know if John Broadbanks made any serious effort to conceal the pride with which he entered upon his occupation of the place. If so, the effort was a dismal failure. After a very creditable college career in the Old Country, John had become a fully ordained minister at last. As he strutted bare-headed up and down the lawn, or lounged in lordly abandon in a deck-chair on the verandah, it was easy to discern the pride with which he made himself the master of the manse. And when, from the cavernous old hall, there emerged on to the sunny verandah a slighter, slenderer form, all clad in the becoming *déshabillé* of blue sunbonnet and print pinafore, it was just as easy to read in his eyes the satisfaction with which he had made Lilian its mistress.

John meant well, and certainly no ministry could have opened with fairer promise. Everything was in his favour. He had good health, a pleasing presence, a fine education, a hungry mind, a lofty ideal, a devoted congregation, and a wife who worshipped him. And yet, for all that, he came to grief. He sinned greatly and was greatly forgiven. The years that he allowed the cankerworm to eat were never exactly restored to him, but I am sure that the later years of his life were the more rich and fruitful because of his earlier transgression and repentance. But I anticipate : I must tell the whole story.

John, I have said, meant well ; but he had one grave frailty. He was generous to a fault. He could not say ' No.' Therein lay the root of all the misery. If only John Broadbanks, in the course of his elocutionary exercises, had mastered the clear emphatic enunciation of that mighty monosyllable, it would have saved that opening ministry of his from sad disaster. But it was not in him to do it. In order to get to the secret of the trouble, you must know something of the place itself. Silverstream, as can be seen from the map, is in the province of Otago. Otago is essentially a Scottish settlement : was it not founded less than a century ago by elders of the Free Kirk? In such a community the induction of a new minister is an event of some moment. Now Silverstream, you must know, is merely one of scores of small townships and tiny hamlets scattered about the Taieri Plain. True, it is among the largest of those settlements, but it is only one of many for all that.

When John first settled at Silverstream, I was at Mosgiel—eight miles away—and I remember how sermon-tasters from far and near visited Silverstream to sample his wares. Good folk from all the distant villages, and from the farms among the surrounding hills, drove over to hear the new minister. It was amusing to see the miscellaneous assortment of vehicles grouped about the church on a fine Sunday evening, the horses tied to posts round the yard, or tethered to the wheels of the buggies they had so recently drawn. The verdict was distinctly favourable. Indeed, it was out of that flattering verdict that the trouble arose. It was inevitable that so pleasing a speaker should be deluged with invitations. The villages were all around ; the city was scarcely a dozen miles away. From city and hamlet invitations poured in. In those Scottish settlements so far from Scotland, the soirée is a great institution ; and at every soirée John was in request. On the other hand, the city held out open arms of supplication. Would he attend this function ? Would he speak at this meeting ? And to all the soirées and the anniversaries and the public meetings John went ; and he always did well. His people were proud of the growing popularity of their young minister ; Lilian was proud of him ; and for awhile nothing but good came of it. Perhaps it was his duty, having friends, to show himself friendly. I do not know ; such things are not in my province. I only know that John was very happy, and very successful, and very popular. He conducted his Sunday services, which became each week more crowded. On Monday evening he met the young people of the congregation ; on Wednesday he led the mid-week service. Two or three afternoons he spent in visiting among his people and it was a great day in most of their homes when he was their honoured guest. The rest of his time was devoured by what he was pleased to call his 'outside engagements.' He would jump up from the tea-table and hurry off to catch the train to town, in order to deliver the speech which he had spent the morning in preparing. Once or twice a week he would hear the sound of wheels at the gate, and, looking through the arching laburnums, would see the gig that was to bear him to a distant township. On those occasions he returned either at dead of night or after breakfast next morning.

Thus John lived a full and strenuous life—full and strenuous and happy. His church was flourishing ; his fame was growing ; his home was like heaven. What more could he want ? But things do not long go on in the same old way. Life is a great variety entertainment. The programme is full of fresh items; and fresh items entered into the programme of John Broadbanks. On the anniversary of his ordination a baby-girl came to the manse; and, a year or two later, a brother arrived to keep her company. At the same time, John found his 'outside engagements' growing upon him. His fame travelled; and the demands upon his services came from greater and even greater distances. Would he speak at Ashfield on behalf of such and such a society? and would he lecture at Constance in aid of such and such a fund? John could not, for the life of him, say 'No'; and yet to speak at Ashfield meant leaving home early on Tuesday and returning only just in time for the Wednesday evening service. To lecture at Constance meant an absence of twenty-four hours from home. Occasionally, when the call was particularly pressing, John would be absent from the young people's meeting or the mid-week service. He did not like it; but, then, he could not very well refuse to help a brother minister. His own people would rejoice that he was helping such an excellent cause. And, besides, it was good to develop the preaching faculties of others in the church. And so he consented. Having done it once, it was easy to do it again, and thus the experience became not uncommon.

John had celebrated the sixth anniversary of his

ministry at Silverstream before things reached an acute stage. The crisis came suddenly, as crises usually do. Like a pack of hounds that rush all at once upon the baffled deer, fifty separate circumstances conspired to simultaneously convince John that he was managing life unwisely. It often happened by this time that he would be away from home for days together. He would leave Silverstream on Monday morning; speak at Grantham that night; deliver an address at Cranbrook on Tuesday; lecture at Haythorn on Wednesday; take part in the anniversary celebration at Winton on Thursday; and return home on Friday. By this method, as John explained to Lilian, a good deal of time was saved. It obviated the necessity for separate journeys to and from each place.

The first intimation that something was wrong came rather curiously. It happened that, one week, owing to a public holiday, and to a variety of contributing causes, John had no 'outside engagements.' To make up for lost time, he spent five afternoons visiting his people! The heart-to-heart talks and sacred confidences of those memorable afternoons strangely exhilarated him. It was good to listen again to the testimonies of the old people, to minister comfort to the sick and dying, and to gather the various households about the throne of the heavenly grace. John went back to the manse each evening with a singular glow upon his spirit. Six long mornings that week he devoted to his study, and the very books seemed glad to have him back again. He was present at the young people's meeting, and not only delivered an address freshly laid upon his heart by his morning's contemplation, but actually remained chatting with the members for half an hour afterwards! Everybody said that the mid-week service that Wednesday represented one of his finest efforts. There had often been signs of hasty preparation upon his Wednesday evening utterances. His people did not complain; they knew how terribly busy he was. But the finished and finely conceived address of that particular Wednesday evening was very refreshing and helpful. And then John actually spent three whole evenings that week in the old manse with Lilian and the children! On Friday he was sitting on the verandah with Myrtle on one knee and Jack on the other, whilst all the echoes were awakened by their shouts and laughter. His wife was sitting, knitting, on the step at his feet.

'Do you know, Lil,' he said, during a lull in the merriment, 'I was thinking this afternoon, as I drove home to tea, that this has been one of the happiest weeks I have ever spent!'

To his inexpressible amazement—women are strange creatures—she slipped her apron to her face, rose hastily from her lowly seat, and dived into the gloom of the hall. A little later, the twilight falling, she returned, with tell-tale eyes; took the children from his knee, and led them off to bed. And later still she again crept back stealthily to her old seat. But it was too dark to knit. Her head rested against his knee. He broke the silence by asking for an explanation of her tears.

'Well,' she said at last, 'I should never have said anything about it. You are the best judge, dear, as to where your duty lies. And, if you are doing your duty, it is not for me to murmur; I must help. It cannot be pleasant for you to be always travelling, and the least I could do was to bear my share of the burden without complaining. But, oh, John, I have been so lonely! And, when I have seen other men come home at sunset and play with their children, my heart has ached for ours. And then, when you said that the week you have spent with us all was one of the happiest you have ever known, it was more than I could bear. I cried for very joy!'

I said that this incident was only one of many. Everybody must have noticed how, when one absorbing topic is on the mind, everything else seems to relate itself, in some extraordinary way, to the dominating theme. So was it with John Broadbanks. The joy of the week's work and the sadness of his wife's confession had started a new line of thought; and, turn where he would, everything seemed to contribute to its flow. He entered the study next morning. He was reading Maeterlinck. And, surely enough, one of the first sentences upon which he came was this: 'Let us beware lest we act as he did in the fable, who stood watch in his lighthouse, but gave to the poor in the cabins about him the oil of the mighty lanterns that should have illumined the dark seas.' Had he been giving away to the poor the oil that it was his duty to dedicate to the lighthouse with whose keeping he was so solemnly charged? Had he become like the fabled Huma, the bird that never settled, but was always on the wing?

That afternoon John met Gyp. He was returning on foot from a distant farm, and was crossing the fields to save time. Under a tree beside a pond he came upon a man in the act of drowning a terrier dog.

'What's wrong with the dog?' inquired John.

'Well, ye see, sir,' replied the man, 'it's like this. When he was a pup, he was all right, and we were all very fond of him. We called him Gipsy—Gyp for short. But now he's got to be a regular nuisance. We're always losing him. He follows everybody. And the dog that follows everybody is no good to anybody!'

That last sentence smote poor John like a blow in the face. 'The dog that follows everybody is no good to anybody!' John begged that the dog might be given to him; and the man, who was evidently willing to abandon his murderous project, was easily persuaded.

'Come on, Gyp,' said John. 'I've been a bit of a gipsy myself. You and I will teach each other better manners.'

Gyp received a great welcome at the manse. Lilian also thoroughly understood the significance of his advent. John soon taught Gyp to follow him and him alone; and for years they were rarely seen apart. And, during the dog's education, John spent more time at Silverstream than, in the same number of days, he had ever spent before.

It was on a Saturday that John rescued Gyp from a watery grave. I happened to be holiday-making at Silverstream on the Sunday, and heard John preach. It was a really remarkable sermon, and I could feel beneath his utterance the pulsations of a great soul. 'Take heed to thyself'—so ran the text—'take heed to thyself that thou offer not thy burnt-offerings in every place thou seest.' I forget the points—I can never repeat sermons—but I remember he laid great stress on the fact that you can widen the mouth of a river until it is so broad—and so shallow—as to be incapable of navigation. 'On the whole,' John said impressively, 'it is better to be narrow—and deep!'

From that day to this John has spent most of his time at Silverstream. He has been there now for twenty years, and was never more loved than to-day. No woman breathing is prouder or happier than Lilian. Their children are an ornament to the manse; and the splendid ministry of John Broadbanks is one for which all his people are every day more grateful.

IV

THE MINISTER'S WIFE

I

SHE was the minister's wife, and she might have been the happiest woman in Asia. As you drive along the pretty old road that winds its tortuous way among the fragrant fields and fruitful orchards that glorify the rich and lovely valley of the Lycus, and as you come suddenly upon the ancient town that seems to be hiding shyly behind the groves of tall poplar-trees, you cannot help thinking of her—of all that was and all that might have been. Very few women ever had such a prospect of happiness and usefulness as had she. And yet, fortunately, very few women have made such sad shipwreck of a minister's heart and a minister's home and a minister's work as did she.

The letter of the Risen Lord to His church at Thyatira is never read in manses at family worship. The minister likes to read it by himself; and the minister's wife likes to read it on her knees when the house is quiet. Those of us whose feeble struggles towards goodness are shamed out of countenance by the finer piety and deeper devotion of our wives, and whose puny attempts at Christian service are often inspired and always seconded by those whose lives are wedded to our own, like to read that terrible record in the Book of Revelation in our lonely moments. And then we give humble and hearty thanks to the Divine Author of that terrible letter that upon us has never been laid the cruel cross that, every day of his life, the minister at Thyatira had to carry. And, when the minister is away at a meeting, and baby is in bed, the minister's wife likes to sit by the fireside and read all by herself that sad, sad letter to the angel of the church at Thyatira. And then, with moistened eyes and a lump in her throat, she kneels by the great arm-chair in which she has been resting and prays. '*O Lord,*' she cries, '*forbid that Thou shouldst ever have to say to my husband about me such words as Thou didst write to the minister at Thyatira about his wife in the days of long ago!*'

II

Jezebel, of course, was not her real name. Her Lord speaks angrily of her as '*that Jezebel*' much as we speak of a man as '*that Judas.*' Anybody who knows the story of Judas understands the opprobrious epithet. And anybody who has read the story of Ahab's queen can interpret for himself the letter to the minister at Thyatira. For, in the days of Elijah the Prophet, Jezebel came into the dull life of the children of Israel like a dazzling burst of sunshine. Indeed, she was a worshipper of the sunshine; her priests were the priests of the Sun. Into the drab commonplace of Jewish experience she brought a riot of colour, a rhythm of movement, a festival of song. Beautiful herself, she cast the glamour of her beauty over everything about her. Ahab's court became a new place; Ahab's palace became a dream of splendour; Ahab's people felt the intoxication of a novel and delicious experience. The art, the music, and the religion that she brought with her from the halls of her fathers fascinated the senses of a people unaccustomed to such loveliness. She swept the nation off its feet. She carried the hearts of the people captive. And, before they had realized what had happened, they had forgotten the stern simplicities of their old faith and forsaken the severe austerities of their old life, and were, with one accord, dancing to Jezebel's music and bowing themselves before Jezebel's gods.

It is only by keeping all this in mind that any man can understand the letter to the minister at Thyatira. What Jezebel was to the children of Israel, this minister's wife was to the church at Thyatira. She came into the minister's home like a burst of brightness. She was all beauty, all vivacity, as lovable as she was fair. She took the hearts of the members of the church at Thyatira by storm. She brought into the church a new atmosphere, a new temper, a new social life. All the activities of the church revolved around her. She was the centre of everything. Her charm and sweetness were felt by everybody. The minister noticed the difference, and scarcely knew what to make of it. It seemed to him that the spiritual life of the church was decaying as the social life of the church was advancing. There was more gaiety, but there was less piety. The thing worried him. And yet, how could he complain? His wife was so beautiful, and he secretly rejoiced that everybody loved her.

And so he let things drift on and on and on, in his easy way, until one day it seemed as though a thunderstorm broke suddenly upon him. He received a letter from his Lord, written by the hand of John. 'I know thy labour, and thy charity, and thy ministry, and thy faith, and all thy works,' it said, 'but nevertheless I have something against thee because thou sufferest thy wife, that Jezebel, to teach and to seduce My servants.' The hour in which he read that letter was the darkest, heaviest, most terrible hour that that poor minister had ever known. It was to him the Day of Judgement. The blow fell, not on the minister's wife, but on the minister. And rightly so. '*Thy wife, that Jezebel,*' the Lord exclaimed. For all the mischief that Jezebel wrought in the days of Elijah the Prophet, Ahab was responsible. If Jezebel was wicked, Ahab was weak. Ahab was to blame. And so was the minister at Thyatira. 'Thou sufferest her,' declared the Lord of the Churches. The minister thought of his beautiful wife, of his offended Lord, of his ruined church; and he bowed himself down, and he wept.

III

It is a great thing to be a woman, and especially a beautiful woman. Why, this very church, the church at Thyatira, was reared by the fidelity of one woman and ruined by the folly of another. Women, and especially charming women, do pretty much what they like with us. It was so ordained. God sprinkled so much beauty about His world that by the ministry of beautiful things He might make us all beautiful. When God makes a woman charming, He means her to charm: when God makes a woman attractive, He means her to attract. But woe be to that woman who charms us away from goodness! Woe be to that woman who allures us from the love of God!

It is a great day in a young girl's life when she

discovers that she is courted, sought after, worshipped; and that men find a pleasure in sacrificing themselves to gratify her whims and fancies. In the cool of the evening of that never-to-be-forgotten day, let that young girl, her fair face flushed and her lovely eyes sparkling with the wonder of the discovery that she has that day made, draw aside from the world and read, all by herself, three tremendous stories. Let her read the story of Jezebel from the Old Testament; let her read the letter to the minister at Thyatira from the New Testament; and then let her read the story of Guinevere.

Poor Guinevere! I should not care to number among my friends a man who could read Guinevere's bitter and heart-broken lament with a steady voice and with dry eyes. When Arthur proudly introduced his lovely Queen to the brave knights of his Round Table, she was so radiantly fair, so exquisitely beautiful, that every heart stood still at sight of her bewitching comeliness. She appeared in Arthur's court like a white rose on a knight's breast. And she meant to make herself the very heart and centre of all the chivalries and courtesies of Arthur's reign. No man could look into the face of Guinevere without feeling that her presence made it easier to be good. Poor Guinevere! Who would have dreamed that day that the ruin of Arthur's court and the shipwreck of Arthur's hopes would have been compassed by such fair hands as hers? We have all wept, at some time or other, over Tennyson's pages. Guinevere's exceeding great and bitter cry has touched us all to tears. Arthur has gone; the knights have been disbanded; chivalry is in ruins. The pale queen rises in her anguish and remorse.

> Then she stretch'd out her arms and cried aloud,
> 'Oh, Arthur!' there her voice brake suddenly,
> Then—as a stream that, spouting from a cliff
> Fails in mid-air, but gathering at the base
> Remakes itself, and flashes down the vale—
> Went on in passionate utterance:
> 'The days will grow to weeks, the weeks to months,
> The months will add themselves and make the years,
> The years will roll into the centuries,
> And mine will ever be a name of scorn.'

And, later on:

> . . . Ah, my God,
> What might I not have made of Thy fair world,
> Had I but loved Thy highest creature here?
> It was my duty to have loved the highest!

Poor Jezebel!

Poor minister's wife at Thyatira!

Poor Guinevere!

Let, I say, every young girl to whom has come the consciousness of her own captivating charms read these stories, and then let her kneel and pray that there may never come to her such a day as came to these.

IV

The brevity of these biblical records is very tantalizing. I wish I knew a little more of this lady at Thyatira. I wish I had been her minister in those early days when she made the great confession. It is a lovely thing, at any time, to see a fair young girl, on the very threshold of her womanhood, take her life in her hands and lay it at the Saviour's feet. It must have been a specially beautiful spectacle in those old Roman days. I wish that I could have seen this girl as she came to her minister and sought admission to the holy fellowship of the Christian Church. I should like to have seen her on the day of her baptism. It was a great day when, with tears of joy and gratitude, she renounced the world and confessed herself her Lord's. I wish I had been sitting near her at her first Communion. I should like to have seen the awe, the emotion, the adoring wonder that illumined her fair young face as she gazed for the first time upon the holy mysteries. 'Take, eat; this is My body which is broken for you!' 'This is My blood that is shed for you.' '*For me! for me!*' whispered she to herself, as she tremblingly raised the sacred emblems to her lips. '*For me! for me!*'

And I should have loved to have been with her on her wedding-day. With what lofty aspirations and high resolves did she become a minister's bride! What rainbow-tinted visions fired her young soul as she thought of sharing his home, his life, his labours! Who would have dreamed that day, that wedding-day, that later on the bridegroom would receive such a letter as that which we find embalmed in the sacred records? Who would have dreamed that one day the Lord of all the Churches would liken that minister to the weak and vacillating Ahab, and would liken that fair young wife of his to the beautiful but wicked Jezebel?

If only the bridegroom could have foreseen *that*!

If only the bride could have foreseen *that*!

But they did *not* foresee it. It cast no shadow over the joyousness of their wedding-day. But let all other ministerial bridegrooms, and all other ministers' brides, remember that the dark, dark story of that ministerial wedding of the olden time is written for their learning, that they through patience and comfort of the Scriptures may have hope.

V

The minister's home is hushed and silent. People enter and leave on tiptoe. The minister's wife is very ill. '*I will cast her into a bed of sickness,*' said the Lord of all the Churches. And again I find the record extremely tantalizing. What happened during that long illness in which the minister's wife went down into the valley of the shadow of death? As she came face to face with the eternal world, did a new gravity settle upon her spirit? Did she return to the sweetness and simplicity of her girlish faith? I like to think that when at last the minister at Thyatira, with inexpressible thankfulness, led his frail but convalescent wife back to the church after her long and terrible sickness, her face, like the face of Moses on his return from the mount, shone with a radiance that, in the old days, it had never known. Her eyes, like those of Mary, were 'homes of silent prayer.' And in all their spiritual struggles and secret perplexities the women of Thyatira knew of no one to whom they could resort with such confidence and with such comfort as to the minister's wife; whilst the wives of the ministers at Sardis and at Pergamos, and at all the other churches, regarded her reverently and affectionately as the mother of them all.

V

ON GWINE BACK TO DIXIE

THAT is a great day in a man's life, the day on which he finds himself gwine back to Dixie. But it must be done carefully, circumspectly, even scientifically, or it will end in bitter disillusionment and pitiful disaster. You cannot pack your bag, put on your hat, and set out for Dixie just as the fancy takes you. As I shall show before I lay down my pen, the soil of Dixie is sacramental soil; and sacramental soil is only to be approached after a diligent preparation of spirit. The shoes must be taken from off the feet. Only this afternoon I was sitting in this very chair, chatting with an old friend who, since I met him last, has revisited the Homeland after an absence of thirty years. He is a Manxman. During his long residence here in Australia, his mother had gone to her rest, but, so far as he knew, his father still lived. He told me how, during the long sea voyage, he was alternately tortured and transported by strangely conflicting emotions. At one moment his heart would stand still, and his blood freeze in his veins, as he reflected that, very possibly, he would find his father dead and the whole place changed beyond recognition. At the next, he could scarcely restrain his excitement at the possibility of again hearing his father's voice and revisiting the scenes of his boyhood. These opposite sensations increased in intensity as he neared his destination. At length he landed in England; crossed from Liverpool to Douglas; and actually stood once more on the shores of his island home. He assured me that as he drew near to his native village he could almost hear the beating of his own heart. And when the old cottage came in sight—the cottage in which he was born and in which his bedridden father now lay—he had to sit down for awhile at the side of the road in order to regain his self-mastery. Tears stood in his eyes as he told me of the meeting with his father; of the aching void which had taken the place of his mother; of the visit to the grave in the little cemetery; and of all the other experiences of those memorable weeks. 'I shall be a better man as long as I live as a result of that visit!' he told me. And as I beheld the evidence of the deep impression it had made, I could easily believe it. But, then, he had been preparing himself for thirty years to stand again on that sacred, that consecrated soil. He had faced all the possibilities of disappointment; he had focused his anticipations on the essential rather than on the accidental things ; and his going back to Dixie became in consequence one of the notable events in his soul's secret history.

But, as against this, many a man has gone back to Dixie and has regretted having done so for ever afterwards. If I am going back to Dixie just to have another look at Dixie, depend upon it I shall be disappointed. Places change : that is bad. People change : that is worse. But even that is not the worst of all. The worst of all is that *we ourselves* change ; and the change in us is greater than the change in the place or the change in the people. When we left Dixie behind us, we brought Dixie with us. There it stands, in its entirety, in that mysterious inner realm which we call Memory. But it is not allowed to stand there like a bee in amber, like a picture on the wall, or like a curiosity in a glass case. It is tampered with. A countless host of queer little imps and pixies are constantly engaged on a strange and mischievous work of demolition and reconstruction. Every day they slyly take away from my mind a little bit of the real Dixie ; every day they build up in my mind a little bit of an ideal Dixie. And thus, gradually, line upon line, here a little and there a little, the real Dixie passes from my memory, and a dream-Dixie, a Dixie-that-never-was-and-never-will-be, is silently erected. The consequence is that, when I go back to Dixie, I am amazed and bewildered and disappointed. Has not Dickens told us of the emotions with which he revisited Rochester? Rochester was the scene of his childhood, and the memory specially delights in exaggerating the objects most familiar to our infancy. Dickens tells how he thought the Rochester High Street must be at least as wide as Regent Street, whilst on his return he discovered that it was little better than a lane. He tells how the public clock in that street, which he had imagined to be the finest clock in the world, turned out to be as moon-faced and feeble a clock as a man's eyes ever saw. And he tells how, in its town-hall, which had appeared to him once so glorious a structure that he had set it up in his mind as the model on which the Genie of the Lamp built the Palace for Aladdin, he had painfully to recognize a mere mean little heap of bricks 'like a chapel gone demented.' And then he suddenly reflected that the change was not in Rochester, but in himself. The imps and pixies had been assiduously at work all through the years demolishing the real Rochester in his memory and erecting the ideal Rochester, the Rochester-that-never-was. 'Who was I,' he asks, 'that I should quarrel with the town for having changed to me, when I myself had come back so changed to it?'

On the whole, however, I fancy that we are most of us the happier for the work of the imps and pixies.

Their elfish pranks may lead to a certain amount of disillusionment and disappointment to those who go back to Dixie. But, then, the great majority of us can never go back to Dixie; and the pixies are bent on conferring the greatest good on the greatest number. Since we can never actually walk the streets of Dixie again, is it not an amiable deception that they practise upon us? Is it not delightful to be able to carry about in our hearts perpetually an idealized, magnified, glorified Dixie? The Dixie that the pixies give us is a Dixie from which everything disfiguring and unclean has been scrupulously eliminated; a Dixie in which everything fair and beautiful has been intensified and made emphatic.

And thus the pixies help us to live in two places and in two periods at the same time. I open my eyes and I am in Melbourne; I close them and I am back in Dixie. I open them and it is the twentieth century; I close them and it is the nineteenth. In his *Roundabout Papers*, Thackeray has a fine passage in which he enlarges upon the incalculable enrichment which life sustains from this capacity for preserving and accentuating in the mind the romance of buried years. We leave a place, perhaps for ever; and yet we carry that place about with us as long as we live. Thackeray instances the vivid recollection, that comes back to him after an interval of thirty years, of his first day at Calais. He describes all the whimsical sights that met his eye, and the fantastic sounds that fell upon his ear: 'The voices of the women crying out at night as the vessel came alongside the pier; the supper at Quillacq's, and the flavour of the cutlets and wine; the red calico canopy under which I slept; the tiled floor and the fresh smell of the sheets; and the wonderful postilion in his jack-boots and pig-tail—all return with perfect clearness to my mind, and I am seeing them, and not the objects which are actually under my eyes. A man can be alive in 1860 and 1830 at the same time, don't you see?' And thus, leaving Dixie for ever behind us, we carry Dixie for ever with us, and Dixie grows more and more lovely as the days go by.

George Gissing was only twelve years of age when Dickens died, so that the two men can never have opened their hearts to each other. This is part of the tyranny of time. It says to one man, 'Stand thou *here* in such and such a century!' And it says to another man, 'Stand thou *there* in such and such a century!' And, although their souls are twin, they can say not a word to each other. We shall escape from this humiliating limitation some day; meanwhile it is terribly exasperating. I should dearly love to see George Gissing and Charles Dickens sitting in opposite arm-chairs beside a roaring fire discussing this matter of gwine back to

Dixie. For Gissing and Dickens represent two diametrically opposite points of view.

Gissing thought that a man should never go back to Dixie. He has a good deal to say about it; this among other things. 'While I was reading this afternoon,' he says, 'my thoughts strayed, and I found myself recalling a hillside in Suffolk where, after a long walk, I rested drowsily one midsummer day twenty years ago. A great longing seized me; I was tempted to set off at once, and find again that spot under the high elm-trees where, as I smoked a delicious pipe, I heard about me the crack-crack-crack of broompods bursting in the glorious heat of the noontide sun. Had I acted upon that impulse, what chance was there of enjoying such another hour as that which my memory cherished? No, no; it is not *the place* that I remember; it is the time of life, the circumstances, the mood, which at the moment fell so happily together. Can I dream that a pipe, smoked on that same hillside, under the same glowing sky, would taste as it did then, or bring the same solace? Would the turf be so soft beneath me? Would the great elm branches temper so delightfully the noonday rays beating upon them? And when the hour of rest was over, should I spring to my feet as then I did, eager to put forth my strength again?' And so Gissing elected to cherish in his soul the picture of the hillside as the pixies had painted it rather than the real and geographical hillside in Suffolk. He declined to go back to Dixie.

Dickens, on the other hand, not only revelled in revisiting old scenes ; he even argues that we should cultivate the habit of 'revisiting' places *to which we have never been* ! 'I never was in Robinson Crusoe's island,' he says, 'yet I frequently return there.' He delighted to stroll along the sands on which Crusoe saw the footprint ; he loved to crawl into the cave where the flaring eyes of the old goat made such a goblin appearance in the dark ; he liked to climb the hill from which Crusoe at last beheld the ship. 'I was never,' he says again, 'I was never in the robber's cave, where Gil Blas lived, but I often go back there and find the trap-door just as heavy to raise as it used to be, while that wicked old disabled black lies everlastingly cursing in bed. I was never in Don Quixote's study, where he read his books of chivalry until he rose and hacked at imaginary giants, yet you could not move a book in it without my knowledge. I was never in company with the little old woman who hobbled out of the chest and told the merchant Abudah to go in search of the Talisman of Oromanes, yet I make it my business to know that she is as well preserved and as intolerable as ever. I was never at the school where the boy Horatio Nelson got out of bed to steal the pears, yet I have several times been back at the Academy to see him let down out of the window in a sheet.' Now here are two opposite ways of looking at the matter! We need not take sides. It would be invidious and unseemly to decide between them; but common decency demanded that, in discussing the merits and demerits of a return to Dixie, we should make ourselves eavesdroppers during the progress of this lively conversation.

It only shows that there are two ways of looking at everything. Indeed, there are two ways of looking at those very imps and pixies who are always at work taking down our real Dixies and building up the Dixies-that-never-were-and-never-will-be. You may argue that their work is good or bad, just as the fancy takes you.

It is *good*—say you? But, once upon a time, did they not set to work, in the memories of the Israelites, to take down the real Egypt—the Egypt of chains and slavery—and to erect a dream-Egypt, an Egypt-that-never-was, an Egypt after which, by a strange perversion of sentiment, the erstwhile slaves hankered continually? It was an elfish trick, and they have sometimes perpetrated a similar one on me.

Bad—say you? But why, if they be bad, did they render Jacob so conspicuous a service? See how, within the realm of his fancy, they took down the real Bethel, the Bethel of his terrified flight and his stony pillow, and they built up within his mind a Bethel in which his radiant dream of the heavenly staircase was emphasized and beautified! And straightway Jacob went back to Dixie. He returned to Bethel and renewed the vows that he had made there long years before.

I forgive the pixies for sometimes exaggerating the piquancy of the Egyptian leeks and the flavour of the Egyptian fleshpots when I remember how often, by transfiguring the most hallowed associations of the past, they have led me back to the old altar that, in the flurry of life, I had so shamefully forsaken.

VI

'WHEN MY SHIP COMES HOME!'

So far as I can remember, I was never, as a child, denied anything for which I clamoured. If, in some modest moment, I begged for a peg-top, a new kite, or a fresh supply of marbles, my request was usually granted. And if, in a lordlier mood, I asked my mother for an up-to-date bicycle, for a green-crested cockatoo, for a gold watch, or for a Shetland pony, she invariably assured me that the coveted treasure should be mine *when her ship came home!*

Oh, that ship! How it tortured the fancy of my infancy! Not all the mystery ships of romance have involved me in a thousandth part of the speculation that I devoted to that ghostly vessel of my mother's. I used to creep off into the dining-room; curl myself up in my father's spacious arm-chair—my favourite retreat; give rein to my fancy; and try to imagine what kind of a ship that ship of my mother's could be! I called to mind all the fleets that ever floated, all the squadrons that ever sailed. I mentally reviewed all the craft on which I had made wild and adventurous voyages in the company of Clark Russell and G. A. Henty, Mayne Reid and Fenimore Cooper, Jules Verne and R. M. Ballantyne. I saw again the triremes of the Phoenicians, the galleys of Greece, the kayaks of Greenland, the junks of the Orient, the argosies of Spain, and the frowning figureheads of the Vikings. If all the ships that swept into my fancy could have met in the English Channel, why, as Rudyard Kipling would say,

There'd be biremes and brigantines, cutters and sloops,
Cogs, carracks, and galleons with gay gilded poops—
Hoys, caravels, ketches, corvettes, and the rest,
As thick as regattas, from Ramsgate to Brest.

But still I was as far as ever from any solution of the tantalizing mystery. I could not imagine whether my mother's ship was a tiny schooner, with a skipper and half a dozen men, or a glorious West Indiaman, with four dizzy masts and an infinite expanse of snowy sail. But after all—I used to say to myself, in a choice morsel of sour-grapes philosophy—after all, what does it matter? My mother has a ship, that is the main point; and some day, the most golden and glorious day in the whole world's history, mother's ship will come home! I had dim, hazy visions of setting off with father and mother in an exquisite flutter of uncontrollable excitement; of the journey in the train to the harbour; of the foreign sailors—including, perhaps, a few pirates and cut-throats—clustering about the quay; of the ship—mother's ship—lying at anchor in the stream; and then of our actually going aboard, talking to the bronzed and weather-beaten sailors, and seeing the cavernous holds stored with the priceless treasures of many lands! What a day that would be, the day when mother's ship came home!

Half the romance of life revolves about just such dreams and expectations. Does not Dr. Oliver Wendell Holmes, in *The Autocrat of the Breakfast-table,* tell of one such illusion that he fondly cherished? When he was a small boy, the sloop-of-war the *Wasp* gloriously captured two enemy ships, and then herself mysteriously disappeared at sea. She was never heard of again. But our young Oliver did not relinquish her as easily as that. 'Long after the last real chance had utterly vanished,' he says, 'I pleased myself with the fond illusion that somewhere on the waste of waters she was still floating, and there were years during which I never heard the sound of the great guns booming inland from the Navy-yard without saying to myself, "The *Wasp* has come!" and almost thinking I could see her, as she rolled in, crumbling the water before her, weather-beaten, barnacled, with shattered spars and threadbare canvas, welcomed by the shouts and tears of thousands. This was one of those dreams that I nursed and never told. Let me make a clean breast of it now, and say that, so late as to have outgrown childhood, perhaps to have got far on towards manhood, when the roar of the cannon has struck suddenly on my ear, I have started with a thrill of vague expectation and tremulous delight, and the long-unspoken words have articulated themselves in the mind's dumb whisper, *"The 'Wasp' has come!"* '

I am ashamed to say that I never now catch myself dreaming of the coming of my mother's ship. I hope that, away in the Old Country, my mother herself still talks of the shapely vessel and her wealthy freightage. I should not like to think that my mother had lost the vision too. I do not remember the last occasion on which I seriously gave myself to the contemplation of the vessel's coming. Perhaps it is as well. The date would have been of interest to me; but the interest would have been of a melancholy kind. For the day on which a man abandons hope of the coming of that ship is the day on which he begins to grow old.

Youth is infinitely expectant. A child can expect anything. I remember, when I was last in England, being suddenly overtaken by a terrific thunderstorm. The rain came down in torrents. When, during a lull, I left the shelter in which I had taken refuge, and walked on up the street, I came suddenly upon a little fellow in rags and tatters, sitting on the kerbstone, holding in his hand a bit of stick to which he had attached a foot of string and a bent pin. He was angling in the flood that poured turgidly along the gutter!

'Well, sonny,' I exclaimed, 'have you caught anything?'

'Not yet, sir!' he replied, instantly and cheerily.

Mark that 'Not yet, sir!' There is in it a certain confession of failure, it is true; but there is in it, much more prominently, a dauntless certainty of success. Childhood never gives up hope. As a boy, I never met any other boy who actually found a pot of gold at the foot of a rainbow; but what had that to do with it? Such an irrelevant circumstance could not keep me and my brothers from setting off in quest of the magic spot on which the many-tinted pillars rested. And all the way down the deep, deep valleys, and all the way up the steep, steep hills, we nicely adjusted the exact proportions in which the fabulous spoil should be divided. And each one of us made up his mind as to the precise manner in which his share of the treasure should be spent. What castles in the air we erected as we made our way to the rainbow's foot!

I lived in an inland town, the town of Tunbridge Wells. There was a tradition among us that, on a clear day, the sea could be seen from Crowborough Beacon—a lofty eminence eight miles away. I never saw the sea from Crowborough Beacon, and I never met anybody else who had seen it. But what —to a boy—had that to do with it? I wonder how many times I trudged those sixteen mortal miles! All the week we would lay our plans for the great expedition: the place at which we should meet; the hour at which we should start; the things that we should each of us take! And then Saturday morning came; and, full of expectancy, we set out. It always took the whole day, and we usually reached home at night too tired to sleep. We never, as I say, saw the sea; and we never heard of anybody who had seen it. Yet all the way, along those rough and dusty roads, we talked of nothing else but of the ships that we should see from Crowborough Beacon. We should see the gleaming sails of great merchantmen bringing furs from Canada, rice from India, tea from China, or ivory from Ceylon; we should see the smoking funnels of huge liners coming, heavily freighted, from Australia or the Cape! We might—you never know—see some great battleship returning from a long spell in the Mediterranean or on the China station! Hour after hour, often beneath a burning sun, we boys trudged on along those interminable country roads, talking as confidently and excitedly of the ships that we should see from Crowborough Beacon as if Crowborough Beacon were but a pebble's cast from the sands and the surf. I really believe that, the last time I walked those eight miles along the winding roads, among the flowery orchards and fragrant hop-gardens of Kent, I was as certain of seeing the sea from the hilltop as when I set out on that fatiguing march for the first time. A cat has nine lives, but a child's expectancy has a thousand.

I have only lost one fortune in all my life, and that was the fortune on board my mother's ship. I lost that on the day on which I gave up expecting it. That is why I hope that my mother still speaks cheerfully of the vessel's coming. I should be sorry to think that she too had been reduced from affluence to penury. I said that the day on which a man relinquishes hope of the arrival of that ship is the day on which he begins to grow old, and should I like to think that my mother had begun to grow old? For shame!

Years have nothing to do with it. A man is young as long as he expects that ship to come home, no matter how many winters have left their snows upon his head. The classical example is the case of Simeon. The story of Simeon always had an extraordinary fascination for me. Even as a very little boy I used to love to hear the congregation sing the patriarch's rapturous swan-song. However dark and dismal the night might be, however tired or sleepy I might feel, however alluring might be the attractions of the fireside, I had but to reflect that the evening service contained the *Nunc Dimittis,* and all difficulties instantly vanished. I made my way to the old grey church; but I am afraid I was not a reverent worshipper. I welcomed the earlier parts of the liturgy only because each, as it came, brought me so much nearer to *'Lord, now lettest Thou Thy servant depart in peace, according to Thy word, for mine eyes have seen Thy salvation.'* I put all my soul into the singing of that sublime song; and when its last notes died away into silence, the service was over so far as I was concerned. So curiously and persistently do childish fancies intertwine themselves with early memories that I find it difficult, even at this hour, to believe that I never actually saw the aged Simeon standing beside the great marble pulpit with the wondrous Child in his arms. I have often wondered why this story, above all others, so completely captivated me. But now I understand. Simeon represented all that was best in my own boyhood. His apparent age was an optical illusion. The charm about Simeon was that, though he had lived many years, he had not begun to grow old. Like me, he sets his heart in boyhood upon seeing one day a great and wonderful spectacle; but, unlike me, he never once, through all the years, relinquished the confident hope of witnessing the fulfilment of his dream. I grew weary of waiting for my mother's ship; Simeon's expectancy never flagged.

It was an amazing achievement. From infancy to age he never once doubted that he should behold, with his own eyes, the coming of Israel's golden age. Through youth, through manhood, through middle-age—the period in which most of us yield up our dreamings—through the days of grey hairs and through the days of sunset, he clung with unwavering tenacity to the certainty that he should never taste of death till he had seen the Lord's anointed. Nobody can appreciate the splendour of the old man's faith unless he has first reviewed the history of that eventful time. For it was not a matter of mere years. Any man can keep on hoping if there is nothing to chill his enthusiasm. But, in Simeon's case, everything conspired to render improbable the realization of his dream.

Let any man who desires to estimate the magnificence of Simeon's faith reach down Milman's *History of the Jews,* and read again the last few pages of the tenth chapter. He will then live in one tense moment through the whole of Simeon's life, and see the world through Simeon's eyes. For Simeon lived through one long unbroken series of national tragedies and calamities. He saw the outbreak of the civil war; he saw faction fighting against faction; he saw the priests warring against the people; he saw the palace fortified against the temple, and the temple against the palace; and yet Simeon believed, in spite of everything, that he should see the golden age! He saw the coming of the foreign conquerors, first the Romans and then the Parthians. He saw his country reduced from proud and patriotic independence to abject and humiliating vassalage; he saw a Roman general outrage the temple by tearing aside the veil and standing defiantly in the awful solitudes of the Most Holy Place; he saw Jerusalem plundered and pillaged and sacked; and he saw the crowds of worshippers who had come to celebrate the feast of the Passover ruthlessly slaughtered by the pitiless invaders. And yet Simeon believed that he should see the golden age! Worse still, he saw religion decay; he saw the temple neglected; he saw the sacrifices cease. But still he held his faith. He never doubted his dreams; he was sure that they would all come true. He sang through the whole of the storm. He was certain that his old eyes would yet gaze upon the face of the Messiah. His was an unconquerable soul.

Did I say that Simeon was the classical example of my theme? I was wrong; and I confess my blunder with shame. What about the Child that

Simeon held so gratefully in his arms and pressed so fondly to his heart? Simeon went to his grave; but that Child lived on. They crucified Him; but even as He hung upon their cross, there was a strange light in His eye—the light of an infinite expectancy—the light of a 'joy that was set before Him.' He ascended to the right hand of the Majesty on high; but even there He is engrossed by a deathless expectancy—'*from henceforth expecting* until His foes be made His footstool.' He has watched the ages come and go; He has seen their superstition and their savagery, their frivolity and their indifference, their waywardness and their shame; but through it all He has felt neither doubt nor dismay. '*From henceforth expecting.*' Serenely and radiantly He has persistently anticipated His coming glory. The kings of the earth may set themselves, and the rulers take counsel together against the Lord and against His anointed; but He that dwelleth in the heavens shall laugh—*from henceforth expecting!* He has seen beforehand the travail of His soul, and is satisfied. He dwells in joyous prospect in the Golden Age.

And so I am back again in the old grey church. I once more join the evening worshippers in upraising the triumphant strains of the *Nunc Dimittis*. I once more seem to see—as I saw in my boyish fancy—the old man with the Holy Child in his arms standing beside the great marble pulpit. And whether I look into the wrinkled face of Simeon, or into the dimpled face of the Babe that he presses so rapturously to his breast, it is all the same. I see that holiness is hopefulness. Those who really enter the kingdom of heaven become—so said the King of that Kingdom—like little children; and a little child is always confident that, come what may, some wondrous day the ship of which he has dreamed so wistfully will certainly come home.

VII

COMRADES OF THE NIGHT

We had come to the End of the World; at least, that is what they called it. In point of fact, it was an Australian sheep station, away in the Never-Never country. The nearest neighbours were twenty miles away. All through that golden autumn afternoon our car had been making its way as rapidly as the condition of the road would permit, between the barbed-wire fences that seemed to stretch from one end of the continent to the other. We had been assured, when we left the run at Seldom Seen, that, with luck, we could reach the End of the World by dusk. Perhaps the luck was lacking; at any rate, we were getting nervous about things. The mists were settling down upon the hills; the nip of evening was laying hold of our ears and finger-tips; yet still there was no sign of a settlement. We were gloomily speculating on our chances of getting back to Seldom Seen before midnight when, all at once, we detected a suspicion of smoke curling up from behind a distant ridge. A moment later we distinctly heard the barking of dogs. Involuntarily we increased the speed of the car, and then, as we swept round the bend of the grassy road, the homestead broke suddenly upon us. We reached the End of the World in time for tea; and tea at the End of the World is a noble meal.

After tea we sat around the great log-fire. At the End of the World they build fires such as civilization never dreams of. We talked and laughed together for awhile; and then the experiences of the day began to tell upon me. The fierce glow of the huge fire and the genial atmosphere of the cosy room, following upon the long drive in the strong bracing air of the hills, proved too much for me, and I felt as drowsy as a tired child. Before retiring, however, I stepped out on to the verandah to have a look at the night. There is something very captivating about a lonely Australian scene by starlight. And this particular night seemed to have called out the whole galaxy of heaven. Every star was in its place. I stepped off the verandah in order to get a better view of the skies. Sauntering down towards the great white gate I discovered that I was not alone. The little governess whom they all called Grace was standing with her elbow resting on the top bar of the gate, and her chin resting on her hand. I hesitated to disturb her, but she turned on my approach, and we were soon engaged in conversation. And either the conversation or the night air made me forget my sleepiness. For she said a very interesting thing.

'I always come out here on a night like this,' she said. 'It does me good, and cures my homesickness. My home is in Melbourne, and I have always been used to the city. But they wanted a governess at the End of the World. They pay well; I needed the money; and so it suited me to come. But, oh, it's so different from Melbourne in the daytime, and home seems an eternity away. But at night this gate seems just like the gate at home. Everything strange is wrapped up in the darkness, so that I shall not see it. And the stars come out, the very same stars that I used to watch from our dear old front garden. It is lovely to see them. They seem so companionable, and when I stand here and look at them I forget that I am at the End of the World. I sometimes think I could never stay here but for them!'

I left her musing by the gate and went to my room. And then a strange thing happened, one of those odd coincidences that stamp truth as stranger far than fiction. At the last post-town through which we had passed I received a letter from a young fellow away at the war. He came out from England to these new lands five years ago; but, when the war broke out, he heard the call of the flag and marched away with the rest. I glanced over his letter in the car coming along, but in the quietude of my room I was able to read it more carefully. And, to my astonishment, I came upon this. 'It sometimes happens,' he writes from Flanders, 'it sometimes happens that we really wonder if we are living on the same planet as that which we formerly inhabited. There is absolutely nothing here to connect us with the quiet life we once lived. But at night-time it is different. One by one the stars come out, and we trace the same constellations that we used to watch as we strolled up the old lane or trudged along the great high-road; and when we see them taking their old places in the skies above us, the link with the old land and the old life seems to have been suddenly restored.' I rather wish I could introduce these two—our little governess at the End of the World and our young officer in Flanders. You never know what might come of it. They evidently have a good deal in common.

But let neither of them suppose that they were the first to think along this line. It is thousands of years since it was first discovered that the stars make an excellent medicine for homesick hearts. Many an empire has risen and declined since one of the ancient prophets was commanded to direct the attention of an exiled and dejected people to the stars that circled peacefully above their heads.

Lift up your eyes on high,' he exclaimed, '*and behold who hath created these things, that bringeth out their host by number ; He calleth them all by names by the greatness of His might, for that He is strong in power ; not one faileth.'* And when, lifting their downcast faces, the captives observed that the stars that looked down upon the land of their banishment were the same as those with which they had become familiar in the country from which they had been cruelly snatched, they instinctively felt that there were ties to the old land that no conqueror could break, and possibilities of restoration of which no tyrant could deprive them.

From time immemorial disconsolate men and women have turned their eyes to the skies at night and have felt precisely as our lonely little governess felt by the gate the other evening. The stars have always seemed to be speaking some consoling and heartening message to suffering nations and to distracted individuals. How they soothed the mental anguish of Mark Rutherford! 'The provision of infinity in Nature,' he says, 'is an immense help to me. No man can look up to the stars at night and reflect upon what lies behind them without feeling that the tyranny of the senses is loosened. The beyond and the beyond, turn it over as we may, is a constant visible warning not to make our minds the measure of the universe. This understanding of ours, whose function it seems to be to imprison us, is manifestly limited.' And, in his *Autobiography*, the stars appear to have been ever his comforters. On one occasion he is oppressed by the conviction—the most distressing and unmanning of all the convictions that sometimes seize us—the conviction that there is nothing in him. He walks beneath the stars, and feels that, in a universe of such inconceivable immensity, there is room for every creature born, and, therefore, a place for him. 'I sought refuge in the idea of God, the God of a starry night with its incomprehensible distances; and I was at peace, content to be the meanest worm of all the millions that crawl upon the earth.' Again, he is aflame with anger. He strolls beneath the stars, and, 'reflecting on the great idea of God, and on all that it implies, his animosities are softened and his heat against his brother is cooled.' On a third occasion he is worried almost to death, and utterly disheartened. 'But just before I reached home the clouds rolled off with the south-west wind into detached, fleecy masses, separated by liquid blue gulfs, in which were sowed the stars. The effect upon me was what that sight, thank God, always has been—a sense of the infinite, extinguishing all mean cares.' The stars had spoken, and his hurt was healed.

But standing beside the great white gate at the

End of the World, our sad little governess did not see everything. When you turn your eyes starward you are apt to miss something. And both she and our young officer in Flanders missed the best part of the celestial vision. For the stars not only link the lonely station on which poor Grace now lives with the great city she has left behind ; they not only link those trenches in Flanders with the tranquil English meadows ; but they link up all the ages. Had our young officer who felt that the stars reunited him to his native village and his childhood's home given the matter a second thought, he would have seen that, along a similar line of reasoning, those same stars immediately related him to all the moving drama of the Empire's story. The stars that shine on the British regiments this evening are the selfsame stars that looked down upon the campaigns of Marlborough and Wellington. The stars that must seem to our men in the North Sea to be sharing with them their long and tedious vigil are the selfsame stars that gazed upon the destruction of the Spanish Armada and upon Nelson's famous victory in Trafalgar Bay. The stars link the reality of an age with the romance of all the ages ; they unite the prose of the present with the poetry of the past. As Mr. Edward Shillito recently pointed out, the heavens upon whose wealth of wonder the average Londoner gazes with stolid indifference are

The heavens, beneath which Alfred stood, when he
  Built ramparts by the tide against his foes;
The skies men loved when in eternity
    The dream-like Abbey rose;

The heavens whose glory has not known increase
  Since Raleigh swaggered home by lantern-light,
And Shakespeare, looking upwards, knew the peace,
    The cool deep peace of night.

Under those heavens brave Wesley rose betimes
  To preach ere daybreak to the tender soul;
And in the heart of Keats the starry rhymes
    Roll, and for ever roll.

I fancy that this was the idea in the prophet's mind. It was not merely that the stars that looked down on Israel's captivity were the same that they had seen from the streets of Jerusalem; it was that the stars that they saw were the selfsame stars upon which Abraham gazed when he received the promise of the future glory of his race. 'Like the stars of the sky for multitude,' he repeated to himself as his eye scanned the radiant arch above him. And it was something for the stricken people in the day of their adversity to rest their eyes upon the selfsame spectacle that the father of their race had dwelt upon with such deep and mystic rapture. When Napoleon's army, under Desaix, came within sight of the Pyramids, the men stood still in breathless admiration, and then, quite spontaneously, they rent the stillness of the desert with a shout of wonder and delight. Here was posterity cheering antiquity; the modern cheering the ancient; the world's newest to-day cheering the world's oldest yesterday. The fine deed was inspired by precisely the same emotions as those with which the captive Hebrews feasted their eyes upon the stars that had greeted the eyes of Abraham. It is good at times to catch sight of the things that abide, the things that filled the first man on this planet with wonder, and that will seem just as magnificent to the man who hears the crack of doom.

Which things, besides being helpful and stimulating in themselves, are an allegory, a figure of things still greater. Life needs its fixed quantities, its immutabilities, its things that shine unchangingly. Was it for this reason that, in the Apocalypse, ministers are likened to the stars? 'Coming home through the wood last night,' writes Dr. Andrew Bonar in his journal, 'I was refreshed and comforted in looking at the stars. Ministers, like those stars, are set to give light through the night. We shine on, whether travellers will make use of our light or not.' The Christian ministry passes on from age to age the things that abide. If a broken heart is comforted in a church to-day, it is because the minister gave a message that healed a stricken soul long centuries ago. If into the broken and contrite spirit of some lowly penitent there flows to-night the rapture of sin forgiven, it is because the minister told an old, old story that has been the light of all the ages. 'I, Jesus, am the Bright and Morning Star,' said the Risen Saviour, in the sentences with which the Bible closes; and tired eyes will rest steadfastly on Him until the stunning tides and shifting scenes of time and sense have ceased for ever to confuse them.

PART II

I

THE HAWKS' NEST

It is a lonely little place—a kind of shooting-box—up among the grim and silent hills. You never saw such an endless panorama of bush as that which you survey from the four verandahs of 'The Hawks' Nest.' The tangle of green spreads itself out at your feet, and stretches away—north, south, east, and west—to every point of the horizon. At night, unless you have company, the solitude is almost eerie.

I

Jack Hawkins was really an excellent sportsman and a capital fellow. Send him up to 'The Hawks' Nest'; give him a sharp, fresh morning; put his rifle in his hand; and he will snap his fingers at monarchs and millionaires. He is in paradise. Keen as a hound on the scent, he will never abandon the chase till, with a flush of glorious exaltation, he has triumphantly brought down the game. Once fairly on the track of his quarry, he forgets that he is mortal. His eye flashes with suppressed excitement. Up hill and down dale he prowls, stalks, crouches, climbs, creeps, or runs, according to the way of the wind and the conditions of the hunt. He takes risks, without knowing that he takes them, that would freeze the blood of an onlooker. He never for a moment flags or falters. He forgets alike the passage of time and the demands of appetite. Hunger, thirst, and weariness are the elements of some other world; he has left all such mundane things behind him. Then at length there comes to him a tense and fateful moment that compensates him for all his prodigal expenditure of thought and energy. The game has vanished over the crest of the hill, but, scenting danger and not knowing its exact locality, it has lifted its head and pricked its ears to take observations. For the fraction of a second that head is silhouetted against the sky. Instantly the rifle leaps to the shoulder; the report echoes and reverberates among the lonely hills; and the graceful creature falls with a crash among the tangle of shrubs at its feet. With a glow of pride that a conqueror might envy, Jack sits down and surveys his prize. And, sitting down, he shivers. It is evening—and chilly. He suddenly remembers that he is human. He feels famished and faint; every sinew throbs with fatigue. The west is all aglow, and 'The Hawks' Nest' is far away. He staggers home with his burden; but, arriving there, lacks the energy to cook it. He throws it down; sits for awhile over his pipe; then goes to bed hungry. He reminds you of the words of a very shrewd philosopher: '*The slothful man roasteth not that which he took in hunting.*' It is worth thinking about.

II

Most of us are excellent huntsmen, but execrable cooks. We know how to bring down the game; but to save our lives we cannot roast it. We are smart at acquiring, but dull at enjoying. See, for example, how a nation will pour out its richest blood in order to secure to itself certain rights and liberties; but the moment those precious privileges have been won, it will cease to prize them! The game is down; why cook it? The experience of Jack Hawkins makes it clear as noonday to me that I must observe some sense of proportion in the investment of my energies. It is absurd so to exhaust myself in the chase as to have no strength left with which to roast and enjoy the hard-won fruit of my exertions. It is exasperating to arrive home with the prey too tired to cook it. Amidst the excitement of the hunt I must remember the claims of the hearth. The field must not lead me to forget the fireside. I must husband strength with which to roast that which I take in hunting. A miser, for instance, is a man who is able to acquire, but not able to enjoy. He knows how to bring down the game, but he has no idea as to how it should be roasted.

Is there not something infinitely pathetic about a story like that of Sir Titus Salt? He is nearly seventy years of age, and, by dint of ceaseless activities and exertions, has amassed an enormous fortune. On a certain Sunday morning he saunters about his beautiful garden. He comes upon a cluster of sweet-peas. As he stoops to admire them his eye is attracted by a snail climbing painfully up one of the sticks by which the peas were supported. At last it reaches the top. It turns round and round; but there is nothing there. It turns, disappointed, and slowly descends. 'It is a picture of myself,' remarked the millionaire. 'I have been all my life toiling and saving, and am now too old and too weary to enjoy the wealth I have accumulated!' Principal Forsyth declared recently that this condition of things is very common. Few successful men, he said, know how to enjoy their retirement. Their long-looked-for leisure, when at length it comes, is a disappointment to them. Many a prosperous merchant loiters about the house in his later day much less happy than when he went to the city every morning. He takes his leisure—as an Englishman is said to take his pleasure—sadly. The majority of such men find old age to be the dullest part of life. Many of them die after a year or two, unable to endure any longer the tedium of it all. And why? The reason is not far to seek. A thing without the spirit of the thing is a weariness to the flesh. A man who has cultivated no fondness for cricket will find a cricket-match the quintessence of boredom. To enjoy the game he must bring to it the spirit of the game. And to enjoy leisure you must bring to your leisure a leisurely spirit. The man who has spent his life restlessly will find rest intolerable.

And then, of course, there is our old friend, Dr. Dryasdust. Now Dr. Dryasdust has been all his life learning.

> What there is to be known—he knows it,
> And what he knows not, is not knowledge.

He has pored over his ponderous tomes until he has ruined his sight and undermined his health. He knows everything. He is a walking—or, at least, a shambling—encyclopaedia. But who is one whit the wiser or the happier or the better for it all? I said that he knows everything. I was wrong. He has learned all things but one. He has never learned to use his learning. It is so easy to acquire knowledge ; it is so difficult to make wise use of it. 'All I have to do now,' says Henry Rycroft in his old age, 'is to *enjoy* the knowledge I have already gained ; the time for acquisition has gone by.' It is one thing to hunt ; it is quite another thing to roast that which we take in hunting.

III

Now Jack Hawkins is a problem. Look at him! Here you have a man who is absolutely indefatigable in the field, yet who is overcome by lassitude at the fireside! He is a bundle of contradictions! The selfsame Jack Hawkins is alert in the daytime, yet inert at night ; tireless abroad, yet torpid at home! What mixtures we all are! What sickening depths of depravity you may discover in a saint! What unsuspected gleams of goodness you may find in the most abandoned reprobate! A good man looks very like a bad man—*if his dinner is not to his liking*! A bad man looks very like a good man—*if a comrade needs a hand*! We get so confused by the sight of bad men who are often good men, and good men who are often bad men, that we grow a little shy of labelling men either 'good' or 'bad.' If your good man is often bad, and your bad man is often good, how can you describe either of them as simply 'good' or simply 'bad'? No man is unadulterated. We are mixtures. As Mr. W. B. Yeats says, 'There is always something in our enemy that we like, and something in our sweetheart that we don't.' And, if every man is a mixture of goodness and badness, how can you sort men into two classes, and accurately tie the labels on?

IV

It was whilst I was revolving this riddle in my brain that the wise man met me with his clever proverb: '*The slothful man roasteth not that which he took in hunting.*' If this means anything, it means that a man is what he is *at home.* However strenuous he may be abroad, if he is slothful at home, you must write him down as *a slothful man.* Home is of all places most like heaven. Like heaven, it is, therefore, an exquisitely beautiful place; but, like heaven, it is also a searchingly terrible place. The lights of home are the loveliest beacons that fond eyes ever welcome. Yet at times those selfsame lights flash through a man's soul like the lights of the judgement seat. Beneath their testing rays there is no seeming or dissembling, no cant and no hypocrisy. The street lights and the shop lights may make base metal look like gold; but the home lights are never deceived.

'What a melancholy spectacle,' says Mr. Augustine Birrell in his *Life of Sir Frank Lockwood,* 'what llchoay name spectacle is that of the wit and diner-out, the brilliant after-dinner speaker, whose features grow grim and his expression sour as he approaches his own door! The wife and children of such a man have no appetite for his jokes, no belief in his humour, no turn for his wit; they soon learn to hate his reputation, and smile disconsolately when congratulated upon it. But Lockwood's home was the place he loved best, and where, when he was minded to be gay, he was gayest. His two daughters need never go to others for the record of their father's gifts; they have but to search their own memories and look within their own hearts.' Happy the man who passes life's most searching test thus triumphantly! You can always tell the hypocrite, old Thomas Shephard assures us. 'He shines like an angel in the church. Christ and mercy are never out of his mouth. He is raised up to heaven with liberty and joy on Sabbath days, and especially on Communion days. But he is *a devil at home*!' The fierce volcanic words almost scorch my manuscript as I copy them. '*A devil at home!*' 'The slothful man roasteth not that which he took in hunting.' No vigour on the hillside will atone for lethargy at the fireside. If a man is a devil at home, *a devil he is.*

V

From a purely sentimental point of view, there is something very affecting about the weariness that robs a man of the fruit of his energy. Take Newman, for example. What is the impression created on the mind by reading the *Apologia*? Is it not the impression of a man who, after a long and strenuous chase, is too tired to roast that which he took in hunting? In the course of his brave quest Newman came face to face with the invisible.

> Keep Thou my feet; I do not ask to see.

Yet he derives no satisfaction from his lofty faith; he never enters into its enjoyment; and at last he forgets his vision altogether, and pillows his tired head on the lap of visibility. He no longer says, 'I do not ask to see.' 'Thus,' as Macaulay says in his *History of England*, 'thus we frequently see inquisitive and restless spirits take refuge from their own scepticism in the bosom of a Church which pretends to infallibility; and, after questioning the existence of a Deity, they bring themselves to worship a wafer!' It is not that they have sought in vain. 'Lead, kindly Light' shows that Newman saw the truth for which his heart was aching. The hunt was entirely successful; but the huntsman was exhausted and spent. He had no energy to roast that which he took in hunting.

VI

Our inspired philosopher has no pity, however, for the huntsman's weariness. He would say, I suppose, that a man has no right to expend all his energies in the chase and reserve none for the kitchen. He who cannot roast that which he takes in hunting is, he declares, a slothful man. *A slothful man!* This stern old moralist would, I fancy, be prepared to maintain that, if any man is lost at last, he will be lost through sheer, downright laziness in some form or other. Indeed, he as good as says that it is only the incorrigibly slothful man who fails to appropriate and enjoy the wealthy spoils of life's great chase.

II

THE UNDERTAKER

We have been very unjust to the undertaker. Our literature has passed him by with a sneer. What novelist has chosen an undertaker as the hero of his fine romance? What novelist has even chosen an undertaker as the villain of the piece? We depict him merely as an object of derision; a creature made up of simulated gravity and crocodile tears; a thing that is neither lovesome nor loathsome, but just lugubrious. Charles Dickens did more than any other man to fling a glamour of romance about those walks of life than had lost their reputations. But even Dickens collapsed when he came to the undertaker. We all know Mr. Sowerby, among whose coffins poor little Oliver Twist used to sleep.

'Mr. Sowerby was a tall, gaunt, large-jointed man, attired in a suit of threadbare black, with darned cotton stockings of the same colour, and shoes to answer. His features were not naturally intended to wear a smiling aspect, but he was in general rather given to professional jocosity.'

Professional jocosity, mark you! And we are not left without specimens of Mr. Sowerby's gloomy wit. Mr. Sowerby had the contract for burying the paupers who died in the workhouse—a course to which the said paupers resorted on the slightest provocation.

'"The prices allowed by the board are very small, Mr. Bumble!" complained the undertaker.

'"So are the coffins," replied the beadle, with precisely as near an approach to a laugh as a great official ought to indulge in.

'Mr. Sowerby was much tickled at this; as, of course, he ought to be; and laughed a long time without cessation. "Well, well, Mr. Bumble," he said at length, "there's no denying that, since the new system of feeding has come in, the coffins are something narrower and more shallow than they used to be; but we must have some profit, Mr. Bumble."

'"Well, well," said Mr. Bumble, "every trade has its drawbacks. A fair profit is, of course, allowable."

'"Of course, of course," replied the undertaker; "and if I don't get a profit upon this or that particular article, why, I make it up in the long run, you see—he! he! he!"'

With that sepulchral giggle we may take our leave of Mr. Sowerby, and we are glad to see the back of him. I only introduced him in order to show that even Dickens could see nothing good in the undertaker.

Whilst Dickens was pillorying poor Mr. Sowerby on one side of the Atlantic, Dr. Oliver Wendell Holmes, on the other side, was adding *The Poet at the Breakfast-table* to the growing pile of American literature. The breakfast-table is, of course, the breakfast-table of the boarding-house; and the poet, after the fashion of boarders, is talking about the landlady. Her prosperity, it seems, does not entirely arise from the profits of the boarding-house. 'Her daughter had married well, to a member of what we may call the post-medical profession, that, namely, which deals with the mortal frame after the practitioners of the healing art have done with it and taken their leave. So thriving had this son-in-law of hers been in this business that his wife drove about in her own carriage, drawn by a pair of jet-black horses of most dignified demeanour, whose only fault was a tendency to relapse at once into a walk after every application of a stimulus that quickened their pace to a trot; which application always caused them to look round upon the driver with a surprised and offended air, as if he had been guilty of a grave indecorum. The landlady's daughter had been blessed with a number of children, of great sobriety of outward aspect, but remarkably cheerful in their inward habit of mind, more especially on the occasion of the death of a doll, which was an almost daily occurrence, and gave them immense delight in getting up a funeral, for which they had a complete miniature outfit. How happy they were under their solemn aspect! For the head mourner, a child of remarkable gifts, could actually make the tears run down her cheeks—as real ones as if she had been a grown person following a rich relative, who had not forgotten his connexions, to his last unfurnished lodgings.'

Elsewhere, Dr. Holmes tells us that he himself might have been a Christian minister if the visiting clergyman had not looked and talked 'so much like an undertaker.'

I need say no more. If Charles Dickens and Oliver Wendell Holmes, the literary princes of two continents, adopt this vein in speaking of undertakers, the comments of the smaller scribblers can be readily imagined. The undertaker, I regret to say, cuts but a sorry figure in the republic of letters.

And yet there are a few characteristics of the undertaker that are well worth thinking about. His name, for example. What delicacy could be finer than the delicacy that denominates this man an 'undertaker'? Imagine the arrival on this planet of a thoughtful and observant visitor from Mars. He walks down one of our principal streets and reads the signs over the shops. He comprehends at a glance that the draper sells drapery; that the jeweller sells jewels; that the shoemaker sells shoes; that the fruiterer sells fruit; that the baker bakes; and that the hairdresser dresses hair. And then he comes to the undertaker! What does the undertaker do? Clearly, he undertakes; but undertakes what? For the matter of that, we are all undertakers. The king undertakes to govern; the preacher undertakes to preach; the doctor undertakes to heal; the farmer undertakes to farm. Why, more than any of these, should this particular man be called an undertaker? There is a question for you; a question that a very small child can ask, but that a very wise man cannot answer.

It is part of the reticence that we practise in relation to certain themes. Carlyle makes merry at the expense of poor Louis the Fifteenth, who 'would not suffer death to be spoken of; avoided the sight of churchyards, funereal monuments, and whatsoever could bring it to mind. It is,' says the sage, 'the resource of the ostrich who, hard hunted, sticks his foolish head in the ground and would fain forget that his foolish unseeing body is not unseen too.' Bishop Alexander tells of a man who was resolved to keep from his children the knowledge of death. 'He was the governor of a colony, and had lost in succession his wife and many children. Two only, mere infants, were left. He withdrew to a beautiful and secluded island, and tried to barricade his daughters from the fatal knowledge which, when once acquired, darkens the spirit with anticipation. In the ocean-island, death was to be a forbidden word. If met with in the pages of a book, and questions were asked, no answer was to be given. If some one expired, the body was to be removed, and the children were to be told that the departed had gone to another country. 'It does not need much imagination,' adds the bishop, 'to feel sure that the secret could not be kept; that some fish lying on the coral reef, or some bright bird killed in the tropic forest, gave the little ones the hint of a something that touched the splendour of the sunset with a strange presentiment; that some hour came when, as to the rest of us, so to them, the mute presence would insist upon being made known.'

We smile at the French king and the colonial governor; but, having smiled, we proceed to do as they did. We say, 'If anything should happen to me'; and we call the man into whose hands we should then fall 'the undertaker'! It is one of the niceties of human speech; one of the delicacies of phraseology; it is part of the compact into which we have all entered to talk about certain things without mentioning them. On some subjects we are all tongue-tied.

I began by saying that we have been very unjust to the undertaker. That is so. There is no valid reason why we should write of him in terms of ridicule, and refer to him in terms of reticence. The undertaker has nothing to be ashamed of. I was looking the other day at a great picture. It was entitled 'The Burial of Moses.' It represented the wild, weird mountain scenery amidst which the great leader was laid to rest. Above one of the crags an eagle is soaring. If I were an undertaker, I should have a copy of that engraving framed and placed in a prominent position in my dining-room. It would remind me that a divine hand had once done the work that I was called to do. Underneath the engraving, of course, would appear the august and majestic record: 'So Moses, the servant of the Lord, died there in the land of Moab, according to the word of the Lord, and *He buried him* in the land of Moab, over against Beth-peor; but no man knoweth of his sepulchre unto this day.'

> And had he not high honour,
>   The hillside for a pall,
> To lie in state while angels wait,
>   With stars for tapers tall:
> And the dark rock pines, like tossing plumes,
>   Over his bier to wave,
> And God's own hand, in that lonely land,
>   To lay him in his grave?

And yet, on the other hand, I am bound to admit

that the undertaker is a fungus, an excrescence, an innovation; he was not in the original programme. I can never read the story of Enoch's translation, of Elijah's flight on the wings of the wind, or of the glorious ascension of our Lord Himself, without thinking that these were models of what might have been, what should have been. The distinction of Enoch was that, in a dark age, he recaptured the glory of the world's beginning. He discovered how men were meant to live: they were to be the comrades of Deity, so he walked with God. He discovered how men were meant to go home, so he went that way. He had no need of an undertaker.

Indeed, it is the way of heroes to dispense with the undertaker's services. Their bones lie bleaching upon some distant desert, or fall upon some confused battlefield, or toss with tangle and with shell in the dark caverns of the ocean. I remember that, when last I strolled through Westminster Abbey and St. Paul's, I was impressed by the number of monuments erected to men whose bones were never enclosed in any coffin. In the great Abbey there stand scores of monuments like that erected to the memory of Sir John Franklin, on which I read the famous epitaph written for him by Lord Tennyson:

> Not here! the White North hath thy bones, and thou,
> Heroic Sailor Soul!

Art passing on thy happier voyage now
Towards no earthly Pole!

No, there was no room for the undertaker in the original scheme of things; some of earth's most valiant sons seemed to have an inkling of this, and they contrived to do without him.

My last word on the undertaker is suggested by Mark Rutherford. Mark is taking a Sunday morning stroll through the slums round Drury Lane. The hideous sights! the disgusting sounds! the loathsome smells! the universal squalor! And then he comes upon an undertaker's shop. 'The undertaker had not put up his shutters. He had drawn down a yellow blind, in which was painted a picture of a suburban cemetery. Two funerals, the loftiest effort of his craft, were depicted approaching the gates. When the gas was alight behind the blind, an effect was produced which was doubtless much admired. He also displayed in his window a model coffin, a work of art. It was about a foot long, varnished, studded with little brass nails, and on the lid was fastened a rustic cross stretching from end to end.'

The cross upon the coffin!

'This may have been nothing more than an advertisement,' adds Mark Rutherford, 'but from the care with which the cross was elaborated, and the neatness with which it was made to resemble a natural piece of wood, I am inclined to believe that the man felt some pleasure in his work for its own sake, and that he was not utterly submerged.'

The cross upon the coffin! What pleasure could the undertaker have found in laying the cross upon the coffin?

'The cross,' exclaims Mark Rutherford, 'in such dens as these, or, worse than dens, in such sewers! It is a symbol of victory, of power to triumph over resistance and even death!'

And so, amidst the most debasing filth and wretchedness and squalor, Mark Rutherford came upon the undertaker. And the undertaker pointed him to the Cross and lifted his heart from gloom to glory. Yes, the undertaker did it, and an angel from heaven could have done no more.

III

'PLEASE SHUT THIS GATE!'

It was at Criccieth; and Mr. Lloyd George was playing golf. It happened that, after a round, he and a friend had to cross some fields in which cattle were grazing. 'I was so eager to catch every word that fell from Mr. Lloyd George's lips,' explains his companion, 'that I failed to close one of the gates through which we passed.' But Mr. Lloyd George noticed it, paused, went back and carefully shut and latched the gate. They resumed their walk. 'Do you remember old Dr. ——, of ——?' asked Mr. Lloyd George, mentioning a local worthy not long deceased. 'When he was on his death-bed a clergyman went to him and asked him if there was anything he would like to say or any message he wanted to deliver. "No," answered the doctor, "except that through life I think I have always closed the gates behind me!"'

There is, I fancy, a good deal in that. I had in my congregation at Mosgiel a little old man of singular serenity of countenance and sweetness of disposition. Nothing seemed to ruffle his faith or disturb the perfect tranquillity of his spirit. One evening, in the early autumn, he came down to the manse to bring me a basket of freshly gathered fruit. We sat for a while on the verandah chatting. It was an hour for confidences, and he opened his heart to me. I asked him how he accounted for the calm that seemed a perpetual rebuke to our fretfulness and worry. He would not at first admit that he possessed any features that distinguished him from the rest of us. But I pressed my point, and at length he became more communicative.

'Well, I'll tell you this,' he observed, 'I've always made it a rule that, *when I've shut the door, I've shut the door*!'

I sat pondering in silence this cryptic utterance. My friend saw that I was somewhat mystified, and hastened to the rescue.

'Years ago,' he explained, 'I used to take all my troubles to bed with me. I would lie there in the darkness with closed eyes, fretting and worrying all the time. I tossed and turned from one side of the bed to the other, as wide awake as at broad noon. As life went on, the habit grew upon me until it threatened to undermine my health. Then, one night, things reached a crisis. I could not sleep, so I rose from my bed and sat at the open window. The garden below and the fields beyond were flooded in silvery moonlight. Not a breath of wind was stirring; the intense stillness was positively uncanny. The perfect tranquillity mocked the surging tumult of my brain. How quiet the room seemed! And I had entered into it—for what? My behaviour seemed absurd in the extreme. I had come to this haven of peace; Nature had wrapped around me her infinite calm; and here was I allowing all the worries of the world to fever my brain and break upon my rest! Why had I locked the office door so carefully if I wished all the ledgers and day-books and order-forms to follow me home? Why had I closed the bedroom door so carefully if I wished all the cares of life to follow me in? I knelt down there at the window-sill, with the delicious air of the still night caressing my face, and I then and there asked God to forgive me. And, since then, *when I've shut a door, I've shut a door*!'

I have often since, when the fret and fever of life have been too much for me, recalled my old friend's story. It is a great thing to be able to go through life, like Mr. Lloyd George's doctor, closing all the gates behind one. Take our decisions, for example. I have sometimes to make up my mind—to buy or to refuse; to sell or to hold; to go or to stay; to accept or to decline. The process of decision should be as leisurely and unhurried as the circumstances will permit. But when a verdict is reached, that judgement should be final. I have no right to insult my own intelligence. I must learn to treat it with respect. There can be no profit in establishing within my mind Courts of Appeal that have no power to carry their findings into effect. Nine times out of ten the verdict of the first court is irrevocable; why then rehear the case? When a man has once made up his mind, let him close the gate behind him, or he will never know happiness again. He has weighed all the evidence; he has balanced all the issues; and he has pronounced sentence. Very well; let it go at that. Why review it again and again? If the decision was sound, why question it? If the decision was doubtful, the sooner it is forgotten the better. Why torture yourself by dwelling upon it? The horse is sold; the house is bought; the contract is signed; the situation is declined; the step taken cannot be retraced. A wise man will firmly and finally shut the gate. It is the better way.

I know that it would have been a great thing for my friend George Cairncross if he had been able to acquire this art. George is a minister; we were in college together; and we have been on the most intimate terms ever since. When he entered the ministry, he settled in a small country church at Langford. The work prospered exceedingly, and he was as happy as any man could be. After seven years the pastorate of the church at Grenville, a large town some distance away, fell vacant, and George was unanimously invited. He was at his wits' ends. The cause at Langford was so prosperous and he was so perfectly content. And yet he was young, and Grenville offered much wider scope! But at last the hold of his own people upon his affections proved too strong to be broken; and he declined the tempting overture from the larger church. So far, so good! But it was afterwards that George made his mistake. From that time forth, whenever the least thing went wrong at Langford, George turned his thoughts towards his lost opportunity at Grenville. As surely as a fit of the blues overtook him, he began to dream about Grenville. In poor George's brain Grenville became enveloped in a golden haze of romance. If only he had gone to Grenville! Oh, if only he had accepted the call to Grenville! In his better, wiser, saner, stronger moments he laughed at this frailty of his. He knew that he had decided rightly in remaining at Langford. But there were weaker moments. And in those weaker moments George harked back upon himself. It would have saved him a world of misery if he could have closed firmly and for ever the gate that divided the Langford field from the Grenville field.

Eight years later, after a most notable and

memorable ministry, George did leave Langford. The church at Bellhaven called him ; and, after another desperate inner struggle, he resolved to go But after the excitement of the farewell, of the removal, and of the welcome, there came the inevitable reaction. Every day George missed at Bellhaven something to which he had grown accustomed at Langford. To be sure, there were compensations ; but George was not in the humour to pay much attention to them. The strange conditions grated upon him. At Langford everybody knew him ; at Bellhaven he walked the streets a stranger. Every mail from Langford intensified his malady. He thought of the people there who needed him, and whom he seemed to have forsaken ; and his soul was filled with bitterness unspeakable. This, so far as it went, was entirely to his credit ; but unfortunately he allowed it to go too far. He let it develop into a habit. Whenever the least thing went wrong at Bellhaven, he convinced himself that he should never have left Langford. It was Langford that now became enveloped in a golden haze. If only he had remained at Langford ! Oh, if he had never left Langford ! In his better, wiser, saner, stronger moments he felt ashamed of this weakness of his. But there it was ! And it would have saved him a world of distress if, when he left the Langford field for the field of Bellhaven, he had closed the gate firmly and finally behind him.

We are expressly told that cattle were grazing in the field that Mr. Lloyd George and his friend were leaving behind them. That is the trouble. There are always things in the fields behind us that may escape unless we carefully close the gates. Who is it that says:

> I have closed the door on Fear,
> He has lived with me far too long,
> If he were to break forth and reappear,
> I should lift my eyes and look at the sky,
> And sing aloud, and run lightly by;
> He will never follow a song.
>
> I have closed the door on Gloom,
> His house has too narrow a view,
> I must seek for my soul a wider room,
> With windows to open and let in the sun,
> And radiant lamps when the day is done,
> And the breeze of the world blowing through.

It is true that my life cannot be divided into water-tight compartments. It is a whole—one and indivisible. But it is a whole, as a fine estate is a whole, with green hedges and white gates conveniently separating one part from another. The gates may be opened and closed at will; but it is good to have them there. We do not want the cattle to stray indiscriminately everywhere. It is pleasant to have some fields from which they are shut out—

fields where the children can gather mushrooms and blackberries without fear. I am very fond of Izaak Walton's *Compleat Angler*. Does the world contain such a triumph of gate-shutting? Our gentle angler lived through the most turbulent years of British history. He was born in the spacious days of great Elizabeth. He was ten years old when the illustrious Queen died. He saw the rise of the Stuarts, the Civil War, the ascendancy of the Puritans, and the execution of Charles the First. He lived all through the days of the Commonwealth; and he witnessed the Restoration! Yet who that has read his book would suspect that bloodshed and civil strife were raging around as he wrote? From the first page to the last, as Professor Jackson has pointed out, we have nothing but 'the murmur of brooks, the rustle of the wind in the trees, the shower falling softly on the teeming earth, the sweet smell of the soil after rain, the shining of the sun on green spaces.' It is a fine thing for a man to be able to shut out the cattle as effectively as that!

Or what about Wordsworth? Was it by some whimsical freak of circumstance that Wellington and Wordsworth were contemporaneous? Was it a mere oddity of chance that a generation almost wholly absorbed in the momentous issues that hung upon the fleets that grappled at Trafalgar, and the armies that fought at Waterloo, should find something very much to its taste in the poetry of Wordsworth? The terrible and long-drawn-out conflict, which ended in the complete overthrow of Napoleon at Waterloo, lasted, with scarcely a break, from 1793 to 1815. Now, singularly enough, it was in the first year of the war—in 1793—that Wordsworth published his first poem; through all these critical years in which the fate of the Empire hung trembling in the balance the poet continued to ravish the ear of the British people; and it was just as the armies of Wellington and Napoleon, of Ney and of Blücher, were being drawn up in readiness for 'that world-earthquake, Waterloo,' that the 'Excursion' was given to the nation. Whilst Europe reverberated with the thunder of guns, and shuddered beneath the tramp of armies, Wordsworth sang of the cuckoo and the skylark; of the redbreast and the butterfly; of the linnet and the nightingale; of the sparrow and the daisy. And to such music all the world listened. And why? Simply because we love to escape at times from the horned cattle, and to roam at will in the meadows in which the cowslip may turn its face to the sun, in which the lark may build her nest among the grasses, and in which lovers may wander in the gloaming undisturbed. Walton and Wordsworth helped people to shut the gate; that was all.

I am writing on the last night of the year It is

an hour for gate-shutting. If the fields behind us contain any creatures that we do not wish to meet again, let us carefully close the gate.

Let us forget the things that vexed and tried us,
The worrying things that caused our souls to fret,
The hopes that, cherished long, were still denied us,
Let us forget!

Let us forget the little slights that pained us,
The greater wrongs that rankle sometimes yet;
The pride with which some lofty one disdained us,
Let us forget!

It is of small use hoping for a happy New Year unless I carefully fasten all these gates behind me.

But the best possible illustration of my theme is to be found in the Old Testament. When the children of Israel, in hot haste, escaped from bondage, the Egyptians close upon their heels, a strange thing happened. 'The angel of God, which went before the camp of Israel, removed and went behind them; and the pillar of the cloud went from before their face and stood behind them; and it came between the camp of the Egyptians and the camp of Israel.' A screen of Deity interposed itself between pursued and pursuers. The gate was divinely closed behind them lest the cattle of the land of Egypt should rush out and trample on the chosen people. And, long centuries later, when Israel escaped from Babylon, and dreaded a similar attack from behind, the voice divine again reassured them. 'I, the Lord thy God, will be *thy rearguard*.' There are thousands of things behind me of which I have good reason to be afraid; but it is the glory of the Christian evangel that all the gates may be closed. It is grand to be able to walk in green pastures and beside still waters unafraid of anything that I have left in the perilous fields behind me.

A while ago I preached upon this theme. An old gentleman, a regular member of my congregation, was present. I noticed that he followed me with the closest interest and attention. Next day he quite suddenly passed away. But, before going, he turned to those about him and exclaimed, 'I have shut the gate! I have shut the gate!' Like that of Mr. Lloyd George's doctor, it was a fine testimony! May my sunset be as serene!

IV

COMRADES

I

On that darkest night that the world has ever known, the night of the great betrayal, there was one man even more wretched than Judas Iscariot. When the traitor rose from the supper-table, and went out into the night, this man kept his seat. He remained in the room, and, although his soul was too storm-swept to permit of his paying much heed to the gracious words that poured from the Master's lips, every syllable of that last tender speech fell at least upon his outward ear. To all appearances he was among the faithful few. And yet, as he sat there that night, he almost envied Judas. If Judas was a traitor, he was at least a traitor branded and exposed; whilst this man felt like a traitor within the camp, a spy being solemnly entrusted with the custody of the most sacred secrets. Yet even a spy has this to plead, that he was snared into duplicity by love of gold. Judas was a traitor, but he could at least show thirty pieces of silver in extenuation of his guilt. He had sinned, but not altogether for the sake of sinning. This man, however, remaining among the Eleven, felt that his treachery had been gratuitous. He had not been lured to it by lust of gain. There he sat in the light within; but, even as he sat there, he thought wistfully of Judas in the darkness without. For Judas had betrayed Jesus; but would Judas have betrayed his Lord if somebody had not first betrayed Judas? And the man of whom I now write felt that upon him rested that grave initial guilt. He was the betrayer of the betrayer. I do not know his name. The Bible is a book of most considerate reticences, most exquisite chivalries, and most noble delicacies; it does not needlessly pillory the offender. This man's identity is never disclosed. But there he is!

II

I need scarcely say that I refer to the disciple who was paired with Judas when 'He sent them forth two and two.' We have all admired the wondrous wisdom of that shrewd, sagacious plan. There is no evidence that Jesus relied much upon conferences, conventions, congresses, and the like. As a permanent factor in character-building He trusted to the influence of a companion rather than to the inspiration of a crowd. He was a great believer in those walks, side by side, along the winding Galilean highways. He attached extraordinary value to those heart-to-heart talks beneath the overarching branches, when the tired comrades camped together at the close of the long and trying day. He staked everything, that is to say, upon the virtue of friendship. He trusted implicitly in the impress of character upon character. And so, all through the ages, He has been pairing us off. He began it when He sent them forth, two this way, and two that way, along the dusty lanes of Palestine. And He kept it up. Here you have Peter and John; there you have Paul and Silas; yonder you have Barnabas and Mark. Later on you have the stories of Luther and Melancthon; of Latimer and Ridley; of John and Charles Wesley; and of a host of similarly felicitous couplings. The Franciscan friars, the Dominican monks, the Lollard preachers, the travelling pairs of evangelists, all furnish corroborative evidence of the wisdom of the sacred scheme. The Pope and General Booth had little in common; but they both saw the advantage of sending out their emissaries two by two. The sisters may wear convent garb or coal-scuttle bonnets; it does not matter: the principle is the same. There is no need to limit to a narrow domestic significance the great primal affirmation that it is not good that a man should be alone.

III

And yet—who knows?—it might have been better for Judas had he been alone. I do not like to say so, but, really, it could not have been much worse. I do not know with which of the disciples Judas was paired; but, whoever it was, Judas had nothing to thank *him* for. Judas would have managed the great business of living—and dying—at least as well if he and that man—whoever he was—had never met. One summer evening the pair of them sat talking together beneath the shade of a great myrtle-tree in a certain fragrant field. Judas admired the great protecting tree, and took a singular fancy to the flowery field. When he had money enough, he said, he would buy it. Did that other disciple—whoever he was—ever revisit that field years afterwards? Could he bear again to sit under that tree and think? For that field was afterwards known as The Field of Blood. Judas bought it, as he that summer evening planned to do. But he bought it with the thirty pieces of silver. And on the tree—the tree beneath whose restful shade they sat together—he ultimately hanged himself. Did that other disciple—whoever he was—ever revisit that field? If so, he must have noticed that the myrtle is blasted and dead; that the grass is tall and rank; and that the stones thrown in contempt by passers-by mark the lonely and dishonoured grave. And as he stood gazing upon that desolate, unhallowed spot, the wind, as it sighed through the withered branches of the dead tree, must have whispered some ugly thoughts to him.

IV

If the Crucifixion had been made the subject of a judicial inquiry, and if I had been retained by the relatives of Judas Iscariot, I should at once have demanded the name of the disciple with whom, in the old two-and-two days, Judas was paired. And I should have subjected that disciple to a severe and searching examination. I should have asked questions such as these:

1. Is it not a fact that all the disciples were voluntary workers, who left fathers and mothers and houses and land, and laid aside all their possessions, that they might follow the Messiah?

2. That being so, may we not take it that, when you first met Judas Iscariot, he was an enthusiast, an idealist, passionately devoted to his Master, capable of splendid sacrifices, and animated by the purest and loftiest ambitions?

3. Is it not a fact that, when the Master paired off His disciples, sending them forth two and two,

you were coupled with Judas? Is it not probable that there was some divine purpose, some design for your mutual good, in the linking of your lives? And did not that comradeship continue unbroken from that opening act of consecration until the night of the great betrayal?

4. How do you account for the fact that, during those years of closest intimacy and constant intercourse with yourself, the motives of Judas, from being spiritual, became sordid, whilst his whole character changed so much for the worse?

5. You have admitted that, at the opening of your friendship, Judas was capable of the most splendid devotion, the most unselfish dedication; you have also admitted that, at the close of your friendship, Judas descended to the most ignoble theft, to the basest treachery, to a murderer's guilt, and to a suicide's grave. Does not that seem to indicate that your influence, so far from helping and inspiring him, was positively harmful and injurious? Does it not appear, on the face of it, that you cast a kind of malignant spell over him? Is it not reasonable to assume that he would probably have been a better man if he had never seen you?

I do not know how that disciple—whoever he was—would have answered these questions. I should very much like to know.

V

I should like to know because the matter is of vital interest to me. To be perfectly candid, I am not altogether disinterested. Like this man—whoever he was—I have friends with whom I daily walk and talk. There are flowery fields in which we wander familiarly together, trees beneath whose sheltering shade we love to sit. I do not wish *these* fields to be as *that* field, *these* trees as *that* one. I am sure that this disciple—whoever he was—no more desired to destroy Judas by his companionship than I desire to blight by my friendship these dear intimates of mine. It is so easy to drift along on the stream of an irresponsible conversation. It is so easy to talk as my friend talks; to echo his thoughts; to endorse, approve, confirm. It is so much more difficult to challenge his doubt, to combat his cynicism, to rally his despair. But, by the memory of that Field of Blood, with its blasted tree and its stony mound, I must import a tang of honesty into our friendship. I must sometimes cut right athwart the current of his thought. I must be prepared on occasions to rouse, to reprove, and even to rebuke him. When that other disciple—whoever he was—saw the field with its rank grass, its heap of stones, and its dead and withered tree, he thought remorsefully of the way in which he had consented to the opinions of Judas when, in the old days, they sat beneath those leafy boughs together. And the memory of those earlier conversations was a torture to his soul.

David Hume saw his mother, in her old age, utterly disconsolate. He remembered that, in the days of his boyhood, that same mother had told him the story of Jesus, and taught his infant lips to pray. He knew it was the doubts that he had uttered that had wrecked his mother's faith. He had ruthlessly destroyed the shrine before which she worshipped. He saw her bow her grey head in anguish, and he bowed his in an agony of remorse. He would have laid down his life that day to have been able to unsay all that he had said. But the fatal poison had penetrated his mother's very heart. She had once believed; her son had flippantly destroyed her faith. There are no back moves in the greatest game of all. The past is irrevocable. The tender grace of a day that is dead can never come back to me. Poor David Hume was revisiting those lovely fields—the sweetest in which our feet ever wander—the fields in which, in the days of auld lang syne, he and his mother had wandered hand in hand. But lo! the bluebells and the buttercups had all gone; the tree beneath which they sat together, she weaving daisy-chains for his boyish brow, was blasted and bare. And when next he revisited the scene, the field contained a mound! I am glad I did not see that other disciple—whoever he was—when he visited, in the field in which they once rested together, the stony grave of Judas. I am glad I did not stand with David Hume beside his mother's mound. But I am glad that I have heard of their terrible and bitter experiences. Their sadness may yet sanctify my own companionship and save me from similar disaster.

VI

I said that I did not know how that other disciple—whoever he was—would answer my penetrating questions. But I do. He would have replied that he was afterwards converted. John, Peter, James, and the other disciples were all new men after Pentecost. That is excellent, most excellent, so far as it goes. But I wonder if it would have satisfied the mother of Judas as she stood beside that stone-littered grave! I wonder how it would have affected his sister, sitting there, convulsed in a passion of weeping, beneath the tree under which her brother once sat! I wonder what his father or his brother would have said in answer to that specious plea! Tell a man whose daughter has been ruined that her betrayer has since been converted, and mark the curl upon his lip! Tell a woman whose boy languishes in a felon's cell that the man who compassed his downfall is now a pillar in a Christian Church, and see the eloquence of her indignant eyes! It is a great thing, a very great thing, for a sinful man to be forgiven, to be converted, to be admitted to the sacred fellowship of the Church which the Saviour purchased with His own blood. But every converted man who, like that other disciple, has stood beneath a withered myrtle, and seen through his tears the stony mound amidst the long rank grass, knows to his endless shame that there is such a thing as *being converted too late.*

VII

Caius Martius, one of the commissioners appointed in the days of Trajan to levy taxes on the landowners of the Syrian provinces, found in the fourth subdivision of Jerusalem a certain field that could not be taxed because nobody would admit ownership. It was No Man's Land. It could not be bought or sold. It contained nothing but the broken stump of a withered myrtle-tree and, just beside it, two mounds. *Two!*

When Doctor Johnson was a small boy he one day refused point-blank to accompany his father to Uttoxeter market. The incident passed. But nearly seventy years afterwards the memory of it filled the great doctor with remorse. But what could he do? His father had been many years dead.

And so, as all the world knows, the old doctor went, at the height of his fame, to Uttoxeter market, stood bare-headed in the pouring rain for some time on the very spot which his father's stall formerly occupied, and hoped that this act of contrition would prove expiatory. Does not a statue representing the doctor's public penance mark the spot to this very day?

When Michael Hebblethwaite was an old man, honoured and revered, he was tortured by the recollection that his younger brother had, years ago, paid on the gallows the last penalty of his guilt. A conviction fastened itself upon the old man's mind that, had his influence on his younger brother been as helpful as an elder brother's influence should have been, it would have saved the younger brother from dark deeds of guilt and shame. Michael Hebblethwaite thereupon petitioned the authorities to be granted the privilege of burial in the gloomy prison-yard in which his brother's dishonoured bones had for so many years reposed.

When, at the long last, Arthur Dimmesdale's conscience fully asserted itself, he went to the public pillory and stood beside Hester Prynne as the partner of her shame, and shared with her the bitter reproaches of her Puritan accusers.

When that other disciple—whoever he was—turned sorrowfully away from the field of blood that was once the field of brotherhood, did he ordain that, when his time should come, his bones should be laid beside the bones of Judas, under the myrtle-tree, beneath whose friendly shade they once sat and talked together?

V

JANET

OLD Janet Davidson—it took me a minute or two to recall the surname : we always called her Janet—had been a widow for many a long year, and the task of raising her large family had proved just about as much as she could manage. They were always golden hours in which I strolled across the fields from the Mosgiel manse to sit with her for awhile when her rheumatism was worse than usual or her cough more than ordinarily troublesome. And often, on such occasions, she would lift the veil that concealed the past and let me peer into some phases of her long, brave, patient struggle to keep the wolf from the door. And yet nobody who knew Janet at all well, or who had even seen her face, would have suspected that she was aware of a wolf's existence. She dwelt in a crazy old weather-board cottage, lying a long way back from the road. In the days of their courtship Alec and she had walked proudly up this road one summer's evening—

it was all fields then—and had selected the quarter-acre section on which they were to build their nest.

'We'll put oor bit cottage right awa' back,' Alec had said, 'and then, if things go weel wi' us, we may be able to put up a fine place in front some day!'

But it was not to be. During the twelve years of Janet's happy wedded life seven little children came stealing into her heart and home. The cottage had to be twice enlarged. And then, one terrible day, the very thought of which brought to Janet's face a shadow, like the shadow of a cloud sweeping across a sunlit cornfield, Alec was smitten down. In the heyday of their happiness, in the prime of his lusty manhood, he was taken from her; and poor Janet was left to maintain the desperate struggle alone. During the 'sair years,' as she called them, she worked half-time in the woollen mills, leaving the younger children with a neighbour. And you should have seen her garden! That strip of land between the cottage and the road was a picture all the year round. What Janet did not know about the succession of crops was not worth knowing. Occasionally one of Alec's old mates would look in on Saturday afternoon and do the hard digging for her; but Janet did all the rest. Very rarely could you see an inch of soil lying idle; she worked it for all it was worth. Later on, of course, the boys shared the burden with her. She lived in the cottage to the last. I am not sure that she would have left it even if fortune had poured its favours into her lap. But no such alternatives presented themselves, and, although it is years ago, I recall distinctly the sadness that overcame me as I walked behind her coffin up the long straight path from the porch to the front gate over the site of that grander home of which she and Alec had so often dreamed.

It was one evening in the early winter that she first opened her heart to me. I had been visiting among the farms all the afternoon, and was making my way back across the fields in the dusk. I had not intended calling on Janet; but I saw her standing in the porch, taking off her apron and sunbonnet, and I did not like to pass. Her sorrow was then some years old; the elder children were at work; her youngest boy was eleven; and the worst of her struggle was over. She told me that she had just come out to fasten the shutters.

'Ah, yes,' I said, perhaps with an unconscious tinge of sadness in my voice, 'the sunshine doesn't last long now, Janet. The sun goes down over the back of the mountain, and the day comes to an end.'

'An end!' she exclaimed, and her face was illumined by one of her radiant smiles. 'An end! Why, my best time comes after I have put up the shutters. The sunshine is all in the evening. I light the lamp and make up the fire and, one by one, Jessie and Mary and the boys come home. And we have tea, and all their tongues seem to be going at once ; they chatter about the things they have seen and the things they have heard : and whilst we wash up the dishes the girls laugh and the boys argue ; and then we settle down for the evening.'

'And how do you spend it ? ' I inquired.

She was silent for a moment, and the old shadow swept her face.

'Would you like me to tell you a secret ? ' she asked.

I said that I should.

'Well, you see,' she went on, 'it was like this. When my poor Alec left me, I had all the children on my hands, and there was still a mortgage on this wee bit place of ours ; and I saw that I should have to work hard and be very careful. And yet I remembered a talk that Alec and I had together when Jessie, the first baby, was born. He was sitting beside my bed with the wee lassie in his arms.' Janet's voice faltered for a moment, and I pretended to be interested in a passer-by. Then she collected herself and went on with her story.

'"Well," he said to me as he sat there looking into Jessie's wee face, "I didn't have much fun myself when I was a boy. It was fetching and carrying from early morning until late at night, and

I always got more kicks than ha'pence. I've heard some folks say that what was good enough for them is good enough for their children; but I should like my bairns to look back upon their childhood with pleasanter thoughts than come to me when I look back on mine."

'"That's strange, Alec," I said, "for before you came into the room I was lying here looking at the wee mite and thinking what a happy girlhood mine was. I am afraid they spoilt me. I had all that heart could wish. It seems like a beautiful dream. And I was thinking that I would do all that a mother can do to make baby's childhood as happy as mine was. It would be lovely to think that in years to come she would look back upon her girlish days as I look back on mine, and bless us as I bless my father and mother."

'And in that very room'—her eye strayed pensively towards an inner door—'we promised each other that we would give our children just the happiest, merriest childhood that any parents could contrive. We did our best,' Janet went on, 'and then, when we had got all our children round us——'

'Yes,' I said, 'I know.'

She paused for a moment, and then continued her story.

'Well,' she said, 'when that happened, I thought

my burden was greater than I could bear. I suppose it was wicked, but I was angry with God for being so hard on us when we were both of us doing our best. And I could not bear to think that now we should all have to be screwing and scraping, and that our dreams could never come true. I threw myself on the bed and had a good cry. And, as I lay there, a strange idea came to me. Once more I let my memory wander back to the days of my own girlhood. How happy I was! Expense was never considered where my pleasure was concerned. And yet when I came to recall the things that were most pleasant to look back upon, I was astonished to find that so few of them were pleasures that had cost money. How I used to love to run out into the fields and hear the lark singing in the blue sky far above me, and the grasshopper chirping in the grass at my feet! How I delighted in watching the changes that the seasons brought—the hawthorn in the lane, all clothed in a single night with a soft suspicion of green! Then there were the fields all gay with clover or with cowslips; the grassy banks twinkling with primroses and violets; the copses carpeted with bluebells; the dazzling glitter of the buttercups; the sight of the rabbit under the gorse and the squirrel up in the beech-tree; the swaying of the corn beneath the caress of the wind, and the flashing of the red, red poppies as the ears bent to and fro. My happiest memories of girlhood were of walks, sometimes with father, sometimes with mother, sometimes with both, and sometimes all by myself, amidst such scenes as these, wandering along the lanes, climbing the hills or poking about in the forest. And I saw, as I lay there sobbing, that, without any burden of expense, I could teach my bairns to love all such things and enjoy them, and to store their minds with memories as happy as those their mother cherished.'

'Yes, but Janet,' I expostulated, 'you can't do this on winter evenings. You told me, you know, that your best time came after you have put up the shutters.'

'Oh, to be sure, to be sure; how I do run on! Well, I saw that other people took their children out of an evening to concerts and entertainments and the like, just as, once upon a time, my mother and father took me. And yet, when I came to look back upon the winter evenings of my girlhood, it was not the evenings that I spent at the entertainments, but the evenings that I spent by the fireside, that I recalled with the greatest pleasure. Curled up in the arm-chair, or sprawling on the rug, whilst mother read a book or father told a story, those were my golden hours. And so I got into the way, even before Alec died, of reading to the children or telling them a story before putting them to bed. But after Alec was taken I took more pains with it. I could not bear to think that my lads and lasses might go off by themselves of an evening in search of the pleasures I could not afford to give them.'

It flashed upon me as she spoke that I scarcely ever met any of the Davidsons on the street after dark.

'Of course,' she went on, 'I had to begin by telling them nursery rhymes and fairy-tales—"Jack and the Beanstalk," "Cinderella," "The Babes in the Wood," and all that kind of thing; and, later on, Jessie would tell these same stories to the little ones whilst I cleared away the tea. And then, after the dishes were all put away, and the little ones were in bed, we got out the book. We began with *Christie's Old Organ* and *A Peep Behind the Scenes.* After that we read *Pilgrim's Progress, Robinson Crusoe, The Swiss Family Robinson, Uncle Tom's Cabin,* and *Captain Cook's Voyages.* It's just wonderful the number of books we get through, and the fun we have.'

She glanced at the rows of old volumes that rested, like honoured pensioners, on a neat but evidently home-made set of bookshelves.

'At one time I used to do all the reading, but then, in those days, I bought the book. We used to make a sixpenny book last us a month. But when the elder children grew bigger, we made a new rule.

They took it in turns to buy the book ; and the buyer had the privilege of selecting and the task of reading it. The boys brought home most of Ballantyne's stories ; and the girls generally choose one of Dickens's or Scott's. Of course, they're getting big now—Jessie's twenty-two and Davie's eighteen—and we read now chiefly for the younger ones ; but I notice that even Davie hurries down the township for anything he wants so as to be back in time for the reading. You would never believe the fun we've all had together. I remember how we laughed over Topsy and Mr. Pickwick and how we cried over Uncle Tom and Little Nell. Oh, yes, my sunshine all comes in the evening, after the shutters are fastened and the lamp lit ! But here's Davie now !'

I turned to greet him, and, a minute or two later, bade them farewell and finished my walk across the fields to the manse.

Janet was not old when she died, although her long widowhood, her trying cough, and her severe rheumatism made us think of her as venerable. She breathed her last, mourned by all her bairns, in the very bed beside which Alec sat with the baby in his arms. Several of the children had married by this time, and nothing pleased Janet more than to romp with her grandchildren.

Donald came to see me after the funeral. Donald was her youngest boy.

'Well, Donald,' I said, 'it's a great thing to have had such a mother!'

'My word it is!' he replied. 'With next to nothing to come and go upon she made up her mind to give us all a good time, and, goodness knows, she did it! If ever a lot of children were happier than we were, I should like to have known them!'

But I could see that this was not the business that had brought him.

'I want to join the church,' he said, after a pause. 'Mother always led us in family worship every night after reading, and she always prayed that we might all be members of the church and adorn our membership by lives lived in the fear of God. I'm the only one whose name is not on the church roll. I've been thinking about it a lot lately, and I promised mother last week I'd join.'

He did; and in the work and worship of that church, and in the organizations and activities of that little town, there were very few movements in which one or other of the Davidsons did not play a prominent and honourable part.

VI

GROWING-PAINS

DAVIE did not think it fair. He was the only boy in the family, and he was never ill. Every now and again Stella or Nancy, Essie or Joan, would develop trouble of some kind and would be straightway ordered to bed. There they would be indulged with savoury broths and toothsome custards, whilst friends and relatives would make affectionate inquiries, incidentally leaving highly coloured jellies, bags of oranges, and glorious bunches of delicious grapes. But Providence seemed to have forgotten Davie. He was never ill. No friends called to inquire with anxious solicitude concerning him. And, which was more to the point, no beautifully moulded jellies, no eggs or oranges, no tempting clusters of luscious grapes, were left with tender messages for *him*. Davie's faith staggered beneath such a strain. So obvious an inequity in the eternal scheme of things shocked his inborn sense of justice. He detected a flaw in the universe. Clearly it was not fair.

But, as so often happens when we bring an indictment against Providence, it was only Davie's patience that was at fault. His turn came at length. He appeared one morning with a glum face and a decided limp. He could recollect no fall that would account for such discomfort ; no hockey-stick or cricket-ball had struck him. The trouble had evidently arisen from within. Father and mother exchanged anxious looks. Did I not say that Davie was the only boy ? He was packed off to bed. The doctor was sent for. Pending his arrival, the medical books wer consulted on such cheerful themes as rheumatic fever and hip disease. The doctor came, said little, but remarked that he would call again next day. Davie would probably have enjoyed the chicken broth but for the fact that it suddenly occurred to him that the school sports were to be held the day after to-morrow. That tantalizing circumstance considerably discounted the value of the avalanche of oranges and grapes with which kind callers had accompanied their inquiries.

'I thought as much,' observed the doctor, when he called next morning ; 'they were just growing-pains. Davie, you may get up and be off about your business ! '

Davie was cheering himself hoarse at the school sports next day, and has ever since submitted to the disabilities of perfect health with heroic resignation.

I wish that all the optimists and pessimists that ever were born could have been made to consider Davie's growing-pains. A philosophy of growing-pains is the very thing they both need. It would put them both right. Here is our friend the optimist, striding off along the path of progress with flowers in his hand, laughter on his lips, and a heart as light as a feather. A philosophy of growing-pains will sober him. It will remind him that progress only comes by pain. The cost must be counted. Growth is frequently attended by suffering. Then, for the comfort and stimulus of the pessimist, a philosophy of growing-pains puts the case the other way round. It comes upon him as he sits—his elbows on his knees and his head buried in his hands—bemoaning the anguish of the world. To him it is like a balm and a tonic. Suffering, it explains, is the natural corollary of growth. Was it not so with Davie? An ancient Highland proverb declares that where there is pain, there is life. It is only through the travail of one age that a better can be born. To the optimist a philosophy of growing-pains will impart a new seriousness and a manlier gravity; to the pessimist it will come like the song of a lark after a crash of thunder, like sunshine after storm. Progress and pain are inseparable.

Davie's proud parents may consider themselves very fortunate if Davie is troubled by no growing-pains but those of the kind that sent him so abruptly to bed the other day. If he follows the normal line of development, he will certainly have others. Does not the mind grow as well as the body? And are growing-pains unknown in that sphere of things? Is not the process of intellectual enlightenment frequently attended by the unsightly and distressing malady generally known as swelled head? The growth of knowledge leads to the temporary assumption of omniscience; and that assumption takes rank as one of the young student's growing-pains. Davie will probably suffer in that way sooner or later. Like the aching in the arms and legs, it is merely a passing phase, but it is troublesome while it lasts. The parents who have reared a family without having been perplexed by the peculiar development usually denominated 'the awkward age' are to be warmly felicitated on their good fortune. Davie's father and mother must not expect such preferential treatment. As a rule, there comes a time when growth proceeds at express speed. Everybody concerned is embarrassed by the rapid transformation. It will be a troublesome time, both for Davie himself and for his friends and relatives. The limbs lengthen by fits and starts; clothes will never fit; life in all its aspects becomes ungainly and uncomfortable. The youth, unaccustomed to his own dimensions, is preternaturally awkward; he is continually bumping his head and knocking things over. 'A rapidly developing boy,' says Dr. Sperry, 'hardly knows what to do with himself. New emotions, ambitions, and impulses come over him faster than he can master them. He becomes restive under restraint, resents the efforts of parents and teachers to direct him, refuses to be disciplined. He wishes to be independent, and sighs for adventure and conquest.' Davie and his parents will alike deserve our congratulations when this delicate passage has been safely negotiated. Until then, let them be very patient with one another.

The entire progress of humanity is punctuated by growing-pains. At the outset we were hampered by no restrictions. The savage can do as he likes, he can go where he pleases, and he can have what he wants, if he have but the strength of limb to acquire and keep it. Might is right; and he knows no restraint but the restraint imposed upon him by his own limitations. Then civilization sets in. Falling under its influence, the savage begins to feel like the mustang from the prairie that, having careered about the vastness for years, is suddenly lassooed and imprisoned and broken in and harnessed. He feels the rein being more and more tightly drawn. And the more refined and cultured he becomes, the more arbitrary are his restraints. At last he revolts. Like Davie limping to the breakfast-table, he is conscious, not of his growth, but of his suffering. But let him take courage. His pains are growing-pains. Like the fees that our fathers paid at the turnpike-gates, those sacrifices of primitive liberty are the penalty the savage pays for getting on.

I have often regretted that Schopenhauer did not apply himself to this matter of growing-pains. It represents the missing link in his scheme of thought. Schopenhauer was a miserable man with a miserable creed. He held that we can never really attain to happiness, for the simple reason that as soon as we gain the height of our ambitions we set our affections on something higher still. We pluck the fruit towards which we have struggled so long, but because of more tempting clusters farther on it affords but meagre satisfaction. But does this prove that happiness is impossible? Is it not rather the way in which we are lured, bit by bit, to our felicity?

I know a young fellow who thought he would be perfectly happy if he matriculated. He passed that examination, and it seemed quite a paltry affair. He resolved to work for his B.A. If only he were a B.A.! In due course he gained his degree; but at the capping ceremony the superior honours of the Masters of Arts seemed to shame his poor attainments. He resolved to study for his M.A. If only he were an M.A.! Before very long he wrote those letters after his name; and to-day he holds a high position in the educational world. Now, looking back, does he regard his repeated dissatisfactions as the ruin of his happiness? Not at all! They were the stages by which he attained happiness. Had his matriculation certificate satisfied him, as it originally promised to do, he could never have become the man he is to-day. His discontent at that stage, and his aspiration towards something still higher, proved the making of him. His mortifications were incidental to his wider wisdom. His repeated dissatisfactions with his various successes were his growing-pains. If only Schopenhauer could have seen that side of the matter, from being one of the most morose and repugnant figures in the history of philosophy, it might have made him one of the cheeriest.

Does not the history of the Church furnish further evidence of the operations of the same law? What are we to say of the ages of bitter antagonism and cruel persecution? That story of rack and stake and thumbscrew makes sorry reading now. We admire the dauntless courage of the martyrs, but we find it hard to understand the pitiless intolerance that sent them to their doom. And yet, is it not vastly significant that we find it so difficult to project the imagination into the iron temper of that age? We look back upon that phase of the world's religious experience much as a man in middle life looks back upon the growing-pains of his boyhood.

The analogy is very close. An age of persecution was always an age of rapid religious development. The faith was forging ahead by leaps and bounds. And just as, when a boy is growing fast, his bones and muscles do not always keep pace with each other, so, in days of swift transition, head and heart do not always work in perfect harmony. Zeal sometimes outstrips judgement. Valour is more noticeable than discretion. Under such conditions a crisis is easily precipitated. The sufferings of the martyrs were the growing-pains of the Church.

Harry Seldon is a great friend of mine; but, quite recently, he was terribly worried about one feature of his deeper experience. He is not as radiantly happy as he used to be. Years ago his faith was a perfect ecstasy to him. He could scarcely cease from song. But now those rapturous and tumultuous emotions never visit him. Those of us who know him have marked with admiration his development in other respects. In all his dealings he is more scrupulously conscientious; in all his utterances he is more considerate of the susceptibilities of others; in all his ways he is more chivalrous, more unselfish, more gentlemanly, and more winsome; in all his judgements he is more charitable and more kind. But, for all that, he often deplores the loss of his earlier rapture. We catch him singing Cowper's hymn :

> Where is the blessedness I knew
> When first I saw the Lord ?
> Where is the soul-refreshing view
> Of Jesus and His Word ?

But one day, not long ago, we went for a holiday together. We motored away through miles and miles of bush, and passed some of our great Australian orchards. After the quiet green of the bush, the orchards, which were in full bloom, broke upon us like a dazzling riot of colour. As far as we could see, it was a glorious pageant of pink petals. Then we plunged into the bush once more, and soon reached the lonely beach by which we camped and fished, sauntered and shot. A fortnight later we motored back again, but when we came to the great orchard country our eyes were not again dazzled. The blossom had all fallen and blown away. I asked Harry if he thought the trees had fallen from grace. Were they not nearer to fruition than they were before ? And is not *the fruit* the thing that matters ? And he saw then that the shedding of the blossom was the growing-pain of the fruit-tree.

VII

THE PRACTICAL JOKE

It was not, I fear, a very edifying experience, but it was enough to set me thinking. I was walking home the other evening just as dusk was falling. I suddenly came upon a lady evidently searching for something. When I first saw her, she was bending down, closely scrutinizing the pavement. As I drew nearer, she turned from her inspection of the footpath and carefully examined the contents of the little black bag that hung from her wrist. She was in obvious perplexity. I paused and inquired if I could be of any assistance to her. She was just explaining that she distinctly heard something drop, when I detected a suspicious rustle and a smothered chuckle on the other side of the hedge. Looking over the gate, I discovered the crouching forms of three boys fumbling with a length of string. On the appearance of my face above the palings they sprang up, burst into peals of laughter, and scampered off as fast as their legs would carry them. The lady blushed;

bowed; she went one way and I another; and thus the incident closed. But, as I have said, it set me thinking.

For the practical joke takes some explaining. It is all very well to walk on up the street, wearing a benevolent and condescending smile, and saying to oneself, 'Boys will be boys.' That is merely a cowardly way of begging an awkward question. Indeed, it is worse than that. It is a tacit defence of the practical joke. It is a recognition of the place of the practical joke in the eternal scheme of things. Boys will be boys, indeed! And what would you have boys to be but boys? And if boys do but reveal their essential boyishness by perpetrating the practical joke, then, quite obviously, the practical joke is a perfectly natural and perfectly healthy symptom. Its absence, in that case, would be matter for disquietude and alarm. It would be as though the teeth had failed to appear or the hair to grow. The development of teeth and the production of hair are natural and wholesome processes. You do not blame a boy for passing through these stages. They are incidental to him. And if you admit that the practical joke is equally incidental, and that he perpetrates it just because 'boys will be boys,' have you not put the practical joke on precisely the same plane as the teeth and the hair?

It seems to me, therefore, that, if you admit as

much as you are in the habit of admitting, you set the highest sanction upon the practical joke, and firmly establish it as a constituent part of the furniture of the solar system. You confess that the practical joker is, like Yum Yum, a child of Nature, and takes after his mother. Now is that true? Does Nature indulge in such sport at our expense? And if, shocked at the bare suggestion, you tender a bald and unqualified negative in reply, you must be prepared to define the precise distinction between the freaks and pranks of the ordinary jester and those tricks and illusions by means of which Nature so often makes us her victims. To be perfectly satisfactory, the difference must be, not merely a distinction in degree, but a distinction in kind. The jokes of the schoolboy must be seen to fall naturally into one category; the deceptions of Nature must be seen to fall just as naturally into quite another. It is not enough to say that the mysterious phenomena in the natural world are capable, on investigation, of scientific explanation. The impositions inflicted upon us on the first of April are capable, on investigation, of being accounted for in the same way. The essential thing about the practical joke is that it has no other motive but the motive of mischief. If the practical joker is to be deprived of his plea that, being the child of Nature, he but inherits from her his prankish propensities, it must be shown that Nature never stoops to become purely mischievous.

Now can such a defence be established? Or must we recognize the practical joke as one of the standard items in the programme of the universe? Is there not a certain elfishness in Nature? Who that has watched the gambols and antics of a pair of kittens can have failed to observe the one's enjoyment of the other's discomfiture? Who that has kept both a dog and a cat has not marked the smug satisfaction of Carlo when he has led poor puss into an awkward scrape? And is not the monkey an incorrigible practical joker? What are we to say of the story of the cat and the chestnuts? Do the Brer Rabbit stories—most of them stories of practical jokes—derive none of their piquancy from their fidelity to Nature? Is 'The Jackdaw of Rheims' purely a freak of the poet's fancy?

> The priests with awe,
> As such freaks they saw,
> Said: 'The devil must be in that little jackdaw.'

It is difficult to see, as long as Nature expresses herself in the shape of kittens and monkeys, parrots and jackdaws, how she can be entirely acquitted of an element of roguishness. And then, as we have seen, there is the boy; and the boy is at least as much the product of Nature as the monkey or the jackdaw. And what about the mirage? The Press

Association, in its detailed account of the fighting in Mesopotamia, reported that in the first battle between the Turks and the British force marching to the relief of Kut our troops found themselves seriously confused by a mirage, the worst effect of which was to prevent the artillery from properly covering the advance of the infantry. 'It seems odd,' remarks the *Manchester Guardian*, 'to read of the operations of a modern army being embarrassed by so old a practical joke on the part of Nature as a mirage.' But there you are! 'So old a practical joke on the part of Nature!' What are we to make of that? Is there not an irresistible analogy between the chimera that mocks the landscape and the trickery of the schoolboy?

The greatest story in our literature of a practical joke is the ghost episode in *The Channings*. Mrs. Henry Wood's readers can never forget her vivid description of the dark night; the timid boy; the silent graves; the weird sense of apprehension; the mortal agony of fear. And then the hideous apparition; the wild scream of terror; the frantic rush, on and on, until 'the unhappy boy plunged into the river, another and a last wild cry escaping him as the waters closed over his head.' Is there anything comparable with this in the realm of natural phenomena? I think there is. I shall never forget that, one day, many years ago, a doctor in New Zealand drove me down to see the harbour. As soon as we reached the bustling wharves a great steamer swung from her moorings and put out to sea. But right in the harbour's mouth there stood a massive, rocky island. Towards this rugged isle the great ship made her way, as though bent on self-destruction. I expected every moment to see her change her course either to port or to starboard, and seek one of the channels between the island and the shore. But, to my horror, she held desperately on. I thought the captain must have lost his reason; I held my breath in terrified anticipation, listening for, and yet dreading, the inevitable crash. And just as my heart was standing still with sheer affright, the ship sailed clean through the island as if it were not there! I turned in bewilderment to the doctor sitting in the car beside me, whose very presence I had forgotten during those tense, exciting moments. He was smiling serenely. 'I thought you would be interested in seeing the mirage,' he said. Is there not a close resemblance between the admixture of tragedy and comedy in the schoolboy prank and in the freak of Nature?

Now this brings us to the threshold of the vast realm of natural illusion. It is like entering the magician's hall of mystery. There is some satisfaction for prosaic adults in the reflection that, if childhood is specially the age of impishness, it is also specially the age of victimization. Nature tricks the child into believing a thousand absurdities. When I was a small boy, Nature was always playing her pranks upon me. She told me that the earth was standing still and the sun and stars all moving; and for a long time I believed her. I was one day invited to go fishing with a friend. As I sat in the railway train, Nature pointed out to me that all the trees and telegraph-posts were flying past me at a prodigious pace. And for a minute or two I believed her. During that hot summer's afternoon I let the end of my beautiful new fishing-rod fall in the stream. 'Ah!' cried Nature, 'now see what you have done! You have bent it!' It really looked like it, and I was terribly frightened. I pulled it out in alarm to see if I could straighten it; but it was not bent at all; Nature was at her tricks again! She was just frightening me for fun.

I have read of a Prince of Siam who was being entertained at the court of Holland. The gentlemen in attendance there told the Prince all kinds of wondrous tales, only some of which contained any considerable spice of truth. The Prince believed every word. But at last they told him that, at one season of the year, the water in Holland became solid, and could be carried about in blocks. The Prince turned away in disgust. 'Now,' he said, 'I perceive that you are fooling me!' Why, unless Nature be fond of a practical joke, does she love to make the truth look so false, and the false look so true?

Of late years this matter has invaded a very sombre realm. It has become the key-note of philosophy and even of ethics. Berkeley held that matter itself is all an illusion, a mirage, a practical joke. 'I observed to Dr. Johnson,' says Boswell, 'that, though we are satisfied this doctrine is not true, it is impossible to refute it. I shall never forget the alacrity with which the doctor answered, striking his foot with mighty force against a large stone, till he rebounded from it. "I refute it *thus*!" he said.' Quite recently Bergson has been telling us that everything—time, space, and all beside—is merely an illusion, a mirage, a practical joke. That is as it may be; I cannot discuss the matter now. But the inquiry that awaits the investigator of to-morrow is concerned with the why and the wherefore of it all. *Why* is the illusion so like the reality? *Why* is the false so like the true? *Why* is the transitory so much more realistic than the eternal?

I remember visiting, in Westminster Abbey, the tomb of John Gay, the seventeenth-century poet. On his monument I read the couplet which he himself composed and ordered to be inscribed upon his grave:

> **Life is a jest, and all things show it;**
> **I thought so once, and now I know it.**

It is not true, of course ; and yet it sometimes looks very like it, just as it looked for awhile as if my lovely fishing-rod was bent. What had really happened was that, like me, poor John Gay had been deceived by the trickery of appearances.

Half the tragedies of life come along this line. We are too easily taken in. I was standing not long ago on the deck of a ship lying outside a certain harbour. We were fogbound. The heads were scarcely a mile away, yet we could see no glimpse of land. Long grey banks of mist lay between us and the coast. 'Suppose,' I said to myself, 'suppose a visitor from Mars were suddenly to alight upon this deck, could I convince him that those long white hills are really unsubstantial and transitory, and that the mountains behind, which are now invisible, are the real abiding things ? ' I doubt it. But we are all visitors from another world ; and we are all being hoodwinked by the tricks and illusions of this one. Time seems so real and eternity so shadowy, the world is so loud and the world-to-come so silent, that we jump to the conclusion that things are what they seem. Paul knew better. No practical joke deceived him. 'We look,' says he, 'not at the things which are seen, but at the things which are not seen; for the things which are seen are temporal, but the things which are not seen are eternal.'

Keen-eyed himself, Paul warned simpler souls

against being victimized. 'Be not tricked,' he says again and again. It is one of his favourite exhortations. For, like the schoolboy ghost in *The Channings*, '*Satan masquerades*'—I quote from Dr. Moffatt's translation—'*Satan masquerades* as an angel of light.' By way of a practical joke a schoolboy masquerades as a ghost, and poor Charlie Channing is frightened to death. Satan masquerades as an angel! Wrong tricks itself out as Right; Evil pretends to be Good! Heaven forfend that I should be duped by such a silly ruse as that!

VIII

THE EXTRA CUBIT

I HAVE often wondered why it was necessary for the greatest of all preachers, in the greatest of all sermons, to affirm that no man by taking thought can add one cubit to his stature. Any dwarf, by the mere magic of his manhood, can turn himself into a giant without tinkering with the length of his bones. That being so, a resort to so very mechanical a contrivance would constitute itself an obvious degradation of his innate humanity. A man does not work out his calculations with pencil and paper after he has once become expert in mental arithmetic. Nor does he worry about the dimensions of his stature after he has discovered that he is made of elastic. He can stretch himself to any length that pleases him.

That is the best of being a man. Without adding a single cubit to your stature you can be as big as you like. Man stands eternally distinguished from the brute creation by his infinite powers of self-extension. He sees a bird in the air fifty yards above him. He cannot add fifty yards to the length of his arm in order that he may grasp it. But he achieves his end far more effectively. The arm fifty yards long might be a most awkward appendage five minutes afterwards; so he gets his bird another way. If he happen to be living in savagery, he picks up a stone and hurls it skywards; if he chance to be living in semi-barbarism, he whips his bow to his shoulder, and the bird falls pierced by the arrow. If he happen to be living amidst civilized conditions, he raises his rifle, and a well-aimed bullet brings down his prey. But in either case, without resorting to the clumsy expedient of adding cubits to his stature, he extends himself by a matter of fifty yards. He does the same thing whenever he casts a line into the depths of the sea. Indeed, he does it whenever he grasps a tool of any kind.

There is an old fairy-story that tells how a stone-breaker, toiling with his hammer by the side of the road, saw a lord riding grandly by. Straightway, the stone-breaker wished he were himself a lord, and a fairy instantly gave him his desire. But he had not been long a lord when he saw a king riding in great state, and he wished he were a king. Again his request was granted. But one day, as his majesty was contemplating the immense force controlled by the sun, he caught himself wishing that he were himself the sun, with great planets at his mercy. Again the fairy transformed him. But one day, as he was shining in his strength, a cloud intervened between himself and the spot on which he wished to focus his burning rays. 'I wish,' he cried, 'I wish I were a cloud, able to defy the sun!' A cloud he at once became. But as, in his new rôle, he was one day flooding the earth, and laughing over its swollen torrents and devastated fields, he saw one huge rock which proudly defied the swirling waters. 'I wish,' he exclaimed, 'I had a hammer and could smash that rock!' And, in a trice, he found himself again sitting beside the heap of granite with a hammer in his hand!

That is always the trouble. Man never knows how great he really is. 'Men hold themselves cheap and vile,' says Emerson, 'and yet a man is a faggot of thunderbolts. All the elements pour through his system; he is the flood of the flood, and the fire of the fire; he feels the antipoles and the pole as drops of his blood; they are the extension of his personality.' Precisely; they are the extension of his personality. And, if he is so elastic that he can make the equator and the poles the extensions of his personality, why, in the name of all that is reasonable, should he want to add a cubit to his stature?

We are always a little slow to see the real immensity of things. We stupidly hanker after the extra cubit. I met with a striking instance of this quite recently. There stands at Kettering, in England, the house in which that famous meeting was held from which William Carey fared forth to India. That meeting altered the face of the world. The modern missionary movement was born; and all our continents and islands have been changed in consequence. The map of the world has been revised as a result of that memorable gathering. The other day a traveller passed the historic meeting-place, and noticed, without surprise, that it bore an inscription. 'I crossed the road,' he says, 'to read what I expected would prove to be a record of one of the most epoch-making events in modern history. Imagine my amazement when I discovered that the inscription set forth the fact that near that spot *a fox was killed* by the hounds of the Pytchley Hunt! Local sportsmen evidently regard *that* as the event of supreme interest!' Precisely! It is a very ancient blunder. A fool may easily mistake a mosquito in the telescope for a monster on the moon. His perspective is all at sea, that is all.

It takes a very wise man to distinguish a big thing from a small thing. A Teacher once stood near a Temple. The Temple looked tremendous. The Teacher seemed so tiny. But listen: 'I say unto you that in this place is One greater than the temple!' And straightway His hearers fell into two parties. A few wise souls there were who saw that the teacher must always be greater than the temple, and they embraced His hard saying. But the crowd believed implicitly in the doctrine of the extra cubit. The Temple seemed to their superficial gaze to be enormously greater than the Teacher; so 'they took counsel together how they might destroy Him.' It was an odd way of proving their point.

Now, having visited in this somewhat abrupt way the Temple at Jerusalem, we may as well peep in at a few other structures—three at any rate. Let us go on tour and visit York Minster in England, St. Peter's at Rome, and St. Sophia's at Constantinople—an English Minster, a Roman Cathedral, and a Mohammedan Mosque.

To York Minster first; and here in this most imposing and satisfying of English Cathedrals we find Charlotte and Anne Brontë. Poor Anne, the younger of the two famous sisters, is terribly ill. In a day or two she must die. It is her last wish to be taken to the grand old Cathedral, that she may feast her soul upon its beauties once again. And as her bright and restless eyes roam around it, drinking in every detail, the impression is overpowering; and she has to be carried in a state of collapse to a less exciting scene. How strong and stately the glorious old Minster! How frail and pitiful the dying girl! Yet I say unto you that there stood one in the Cathedral that day who was greater than the Minster! For what, after all, was the enormous fabric, with all its towers and pinnacles, its aisles and its altars, its dreamy architecture and its storied windows, compared with the beautiful soul of the poor consumptive girl who passed out of its portals to die?

To St. Peter's at Rome—one of the triumphs of the builder's art. The mind is bewildered by its vastness and its splendour. It has been said that an army could be lost within its precincts. And here, not far away from the Eternal City, is old Dr. Thomas Guthrie, of Glasgow. He has left for awhile the imposing monuments and masterpieces of Imperial Rome to delight himself in the sequestered valleys that lie beyond the Seven Hills. He is revelling among the wild flowers—the narcissus, the columbine, the lavender, the primula, the asphodel, the gentian, and a hundred other lovely blossoms that lift their radiant faces to the soft Italian skies. And as he peeps among the dainty petals, and breathes their delicious perfume, he finds himself exclaiming, 'What, compared with these, is St. Peter's? How paltry its dome! How poor its marbles!' The startling statement in the Temple is getting wonderfully believable now. The petals of the wild flowers are greater than the portals of the wondrous fabric! But let us finish our tour.

To St. Sophia's at Constantinople then, under the

conduct of no less distinguished a guide than Edmund Gibbon. We catch our breath as we pass, under his leadership, amidst the stateliness and splendour of the ancient church. 'The enthusiast who entered the dome of St. Sophia,' he says, 'might be tempted to suppose that it was the residence, or even the workmanship, of Deity.' But he hastens to add: 'Yet how dull is the artifice, how insignificant the labour, if it be compared with the vilest insect that crawls upon the surface of the temple!' It is to this tiny insect, so fearfully and wonderfully made, that our great historian points as he says, 'There standeth one among you who is greater than the mosque!' It is easy now to return, and to return with contrite and believing hearts, to the Teacher in the Temple.

Yes, with believing hearts. For, at the end of our tour, the Temple looks so tiny, and the Teacher so tremendous. Since His hard saying was first uttered, the Temple has gone to dust and ashes; the Teacher has brought the world to His feet. Take *Him* from *it,* and you have nothing left. Take *it* from *Him,* and you have subtracted nothing.

Beyond the shadow of a doubt the test of the extra cubit is the most crucial test in life. For see! We have just visited the four stateliest edifices that the eyes of man have ever seen; and we have discovered that compared with the Teacher in the

Temple, or even with the soul of a dying girl, or even with the wildest flowers of the forest, or even with the vilest insect that crawls upon the rugged wall, their splendours pale into absolute insignificance. We must worship bulk and bigness no more. So many stare at the big; so few discern the really beautiful. So many hanker after the extra cubit; so few perceive the infinite extensibility of man. So many people explore mosques and cathedrals and minsters and temples; so few see the wonders of an insect's wing; the loveliness of a lily's petal, the charm of a gracious soul; and—ah, yes!—so very few fall in love with the chiefest among ten thousand and the altogether lovely! But the wise understand! Bulk never deceives them. They scorn the extra cubit. They know the secret of the microscope.

What, therefore, do we want with extra cubits? You cannot state a man's greatness in the terms of a foot-rule. He has within himself an infinite capacity for self-extension. And the higher the plane on which you inspect him, the less the cubit has to do with it. What, for example, have cubits to do with the Kingdom of God? A little child is the supreme standard of attainment there—a *little* child! And, just because cubits are out of court, Paul argues that the entire citizenship of the new kingdom may attain to the maximum stature. No dwarfs; no midgets; no pigmies anywhere! None are short and stunted; all are stately and stalwart! Without any addition of extra cubits, we may all come up to the standard. 'For unto every one of us,' he says, '*unto every one of us* is given grace to grow!'

How much grace? Listen! 'To each of us is given grace according to the measure of the munificence of Christ.'

How much growth? Listen! 'Till we all come to the measure of the stature of the fullness of Christ.'

Grace to grow! Grace unstinted and growth unstunted! Who would worry about the extra cubit after *that?*

IX

GOSSIP

LET no man smile. The subject to which I now address myself is no trivial one. We are approaching a theme of first-class importance. One has only to look up a good etymological dictionary in order to discover that the very word 'gossip' is one of the most sacred and solemn compositions in our vocabulary. Its first two letters are an abbreviation of that august Name that no thoughtful man ever mentions without reverence. Let us take our shoes from off our feet, for the place whereon we stand is holy ground. Gossip may be a matter of life or of death.

'Do you think, Catherine,' asked Mrs. Cardew, taking her friend's hand in hers, 'do you think I could *learn how to talk*?'

It seemed an innocent enough question on the face of it; but those who have read Mark Rutherford's great story know that the unutterable anguish of a stricken soul vibrated through every syllable. Poor Mrs. Cardew felt that she and her husband were drifting apart. He lived in one world and she in another. It is the tragedy that Tennyson describes in *In Memoriam*:

> He thrids the labyrinth of the mind,
> He reads the secret of the star,
> He seems so near and yet so far,
> He looks so cold: she thinks him kind.
>
> She keeps the gift of years before,
> A withered violet is her bliss:
> She knows not what his greatness is,
> For that, for all, she loves him more.
>
> For him she plays, to him she sings
> Of early faith and plighted vows;
> She knows but matters of the house,
> And he, he knows a thousand things.
>
> Her faith is fixt and cannot move,
> She darkly feels him great and wise,
> She dwells on him with faithful eyes,
> 'I cannot understand: I love.'

Mrs. Cardew felt that, if only her talk could match her husband's talk, their souls would once more rush to each other as in the sweet old days of their courtship. But was it possible? 'Do you think I could learn how to talk?'

Or, look at the matter from another angle. Captain Ejnar Mikkelsen, the Danish explorer, has recently paid an eloquent testimony to the practical value of gossip. Captain Mikkelsen was entrusted, as all the world knows, with the charge of the expedition sent out to recover the bodies of Mylius

Erichsen, Hagen, and the Greenlander, Brorlund. Captain Mikkelsen, accompanied by Engineer Iversen, left the main party in June, 1909, and plunged into the snowy silences of the far North. For nearly two years and a half nothing further was heard of them. Indeed, the wonder is that they escaped with their lives. Death many times stared them in the face; and on one memorable occasion they had shot their last dog and eaten the last morsel that their little store could furnish. But the captain tells us that the most trying of the ordeals through which he and his brave companions passed was neither the paralysing intensity of the Arctic cold, nor the increasing anxiety about provisions, but the weird silence and the maddening monotony of the snowy desolations amidst which those interminable months were passed. 'Our only remedy,' continues the captain, 'was talk, talk, talk, and plenty of it. Iversen and I discussed continually subjects that would never have interested us under any other conditions.' Captain Mikkelsen doubts whether either of them would have escaped with sound minds but for the stimulus and relief that this constant flow of cheerful conversation perennially afforded them.

These two witnesses—Mrs. Cardew and Captain Mikkelsen—prove conclusively that we have embarked upon no trivial theme.

'Gossip may be a matter of life or of death!' I said just now.

'It may be more than that,' says Captain Mikkelsen; 'it may be a matter of sanity or insanity!'

'It may be more even than that,' adds poor Mrs. Cardew; but Mrs. Cardew bursts into tears before she can explain how that can be.

I have often heard old men say that we cannot talk nowadays as our grandfathers did. 'You don't know what it is,' a revered grey-beard said to me the other day, 'to sit down and talk. There is nothing in what you say. Somebody asks somebody else what he thinks of such and such a thing. He replies that it is very good, and the matter drops. Then in desperation somebody tells a story; somebody else caps it; and thus a spurious imitation of our old-fashioned gossip is made to do duty as a wretched substitute. But it isn't the real thing. No, no; you don't know how to talk!'

The impeachment deserves investigation. Is it true that we are losing the knack of talking well? Is the art of good conversation, which loomed so largely in the intellectual development of an earlier and more leisurely age, falling into decay?

Dr. Johnson had a pitiless way of judging the intelligence of the company in which he chanced to find himself by the quality of their conversation; and those discussions in which Reynolds and Garrick,

Gibbon and Goldsmith, Burke and the great doctor himself took part were kept up to high-water mark, without forfeiting anything of their ease and informality, by the commanding influence of the great lexicographer's extraordinary personality. 'There is great solace in talk,' the doctor used to say; 'we have minds, memories, varied experiences, different opinions. Let us stretch out our legs and talk!' And those who, with Boswell's help, have cultivated the doctor's intimate acquaintance, will recall the way in which his companions winced when, after an aimless and desultory chatter, their leader would turn from them with a grunt and a scowl of ineffable disgust. 'It was a very pretty company,' he would remark, 'and plenty of talk; but there was no real conversation; nothing was discussed.'

Now, say what you will about it, gossip is one of the real luxuries of life. Abuse it to your heart's content, but it still remains true that there are few things more delightful than a good talk. Go for a walk with your friend, and, when the wholesome exercise and the rich open air have set your blood bounding vigorously through your veins, you find that the exhilaration loosens your tongue; and what feast can compare with the chat that then ensues? Or sit beside a fire, and when the cheerful flame has cast a similar charm over your spirit, what confidences, what criticisms, what confessions ensue!

But we must come to closer grips. As a rule, one great law holds true. It is this: when you have discovered something essentially human, you have generally discovered something essentially divine. I mean that if a thing appeals to the inmost heart of a man, if it lays a resistless hand upon his strongest affections, if it breaks up the very depths and fountains of his soul, it is because it was devised and ordained for that very purpose. If a thing touches my spirit to the very quick, it is because it was divinely designed so to do. Here, then, is the sanction of gossip. We all love gossip, revel in it, find our souls becoming involuntarily aroused and inflamed as we indulge in it. Is it not probable, therefore, that gossip is a divine institution, of heavenly origin, sent into the world on high and sacramental service?

The classical instance is, of course, the story of John Bunyan and the three or four poor women sitting in the sun. Dr. Alexander Whyte says that 'the husbands of those women were away at their work; their children were off to school; their beds were all made, and their floors were all swept, and they all came out, as if one spirit had moved them, and they met and sat down on a doorstep together to enjoy for a little the forenoon sun. And they plunged immediately into their old subject: God and their own souls. And even when the young tinker came along with his satchel of tools on his shoulder, and stopped and leaned against the door-post beside them, they did not much mind him, but went on with the things of God that so possessed them.' Bunyan never forgot the gossip he heard that day. 'I heard,' he says, 'I heard but I understood not, for they were far above, out of my reach. Their talk was about a new birth, the work of God on their hearts, also how they were convinced of their miserable state by nature. They talked how God had visited their souls with His love in the Lord Jesus, and with what words and promises they had been refreshed, comforted, and supported against the temptations of the devil. And methought they spake as if joy did make them speak; they spake with such pleasantness of Scripture language, and with such appearance of grace in all they said, that they were to me as if they had found a new world, as if they were people that dwelt alone and were not to be reckoned amongst their neighbours.' Nobody can think of that little knot of poor women sitting together that spring morning without feeling that there is a place for gossip under the sun.

No man is better than his gossip. He may preach like an archangel; he may work like a Trojan; he may sing like a Gabriel; he may give like a prince. But it is by his gossip that he must be judged. It is in his gossip that the man himself stands revealed.

When he sits in congenial company, when the fire crackles on the hearth, when he stretches out his legs and talks, it is then that you have the measure of the man. If his gossip is questionable, you may be sure that the canker-worm is in his soul. If his gossip is elevating, you may be sure that his heart is in the right place. If his gossip, being free of all suspicion of artificiality and sanctimoniousness, is nevertheless sacred and beautiful, you may know him at once for a saint.

The Old Testament closes with a lovely picture. In those dark days of rapid national declension and spiritual decay, we are told that 'they that feared the Lord spake often one to another, and the Lord hearkened and heard it, and a book of remembrance was written before Him for them that feared the Lord and that thought upon His name.' If that graceful record means anything, it means that One august Eavesdropper overhears all our familiar chatter and easy gossip; that by our gossip He can most readily tell those who really fear His name; and that earth becomes heaven to Him when He overhears a talk like that which John Bunyan heard from the four poor women on the doorstep. I said in setting out that my theme was no trivial one, and I fancy I have proved my case.

X

THE CONVALESCENT

We were strolling through the Art Gallery at Geelong, a friend and I, when Mr. Louis Pomey's picture, 'The Convalescent,' captivated our attention. It represents a young wife who, evidently after a long and dangerous illness, has been able to return to the sitting-room for the first time. The face is wan and pale; her limbs are supported by hassocks and cushions; but the joy of emancipation is written upon every feature of her countenance. Her husband stands proudly beside her, happy and thankful. And the members of the household, gathered about the room, are sharing the general gladness. It is an exhilarating picture; and one that makes you feel on the best of terms with a world in which such things can happen. And it reminded me of a pair of experiences that came to me the other day.

In the afternoon, as I was returning from a round of visitation, I witnessed a scene that struck me as very beautiful and very pathetic. I was passing a private hospital. Outside, a motor-car was waiting, the chauffeur standing on the pavement beside it, holding the door wide open. I glanced in the direction in which he was gazing, and just inside the gate, coming slowly down the gravel walk, I saw a frail young girl being assisted from the verandah to the car by a trim little nurse on one side, and a lady —evidently the patient's mother—on the other. I have seen many happy faces in my time, but I never saw a countenance more suffused with delight than was that of this frail young girl. Her eyes sparkled; her cheeks were flushed with excitement; and, although she could only walk by leaning hard on nurse and mother, her feet were trying to run in spite of her for very joy of going home. Had I but Mr. Pomey's skill, I could have painted a second picture bearing the same title.

In the evening of the same day I heard the Rev. Charles Winterton, of St. Mark's, inveighing heavily against half-and-half things. He was preaching on the lukewarm church at Laodicea, and he soundly rated all things that are betwixt and between. He poured out the vials of his indignation on all half-hearted people, on all statesmen who adopt half-measures, on all men who find refuge in compromise. But he was too sweeping, as people who indulge in denunciation usually are. There is a place in this world for half-things. I am sure that Mr. Winterton could not have gazed upon Mr. Pomey's picture at Geelong, or on the scene that I witnessed outside the private hospital, without recognizing that there are periods of transition that are in themselves more delightful than either the state that lies behind or the state that lies before. Convalescence is infinitely more enjoyable than health. The delicious consciousness of having turned the corner and of being on the high-road to recovery is one of the most intoxicating experiences that ever come to us. Health is commonplace ; and it is proverbial that we do not appreciate it when we possess it. But, so far from being commonplace, convalescence is sensational. The long and dangerous sickness is past ; the issue no longer hangs in the balance ; the patient can once more enjoy ordinary fare ; he can again breathe the rich, fresh air ; he can indulge in conversation and laughter with his friends. Each day he can do things that were the day before impossible to him ; and he exults in the sense of his returning powers. To be sure, he is not yet strong ; a child could easily overthrow him. But, on the other hand, he is no longer ill. His high summer-time of pulsing life and bounding vigour has yet to come ; but the languishing winter of his suffering is behind him, and every hour brings him nearer to the good time coming. He is discovering that there are periods of transition that are immensely more enjoyable than either the phase behind or the phase before.

Are half things really as bad as Mr. Winterton represented? Surely not! What about half-crowns? If the love of money is the root of all evil, I am afraid that I must be wicked above all men on the face of the earth. For I confess that I am passionately fond of half-crowns, although I have yet to discover that I have contracted any harm in consequence of that devotion. I regard the half-crown as a really noble coin. There is something exhilarating in feeling a few of them jingling together in your pocket. I fancy myself immensely richer with four half-crowns than with a ten-shilling note. Compared with the half-crown, a two-shilling piece is quite a poor relation, a second-class passenger. I rarely walk the streets with my hand in my pocket; but if a few half-crowns lie concealed there, the temptation is sometimes too much for me. They are fine things to feel. I should think twice about buying a thing if the purchase would involve me in the surrender of the last half-crown I had about me. Yet a whole crown is an abomination. A five-shilling piece is about as awkward, as clumsy, as unattractive a coin as one need wish to handle. Every attempt to popularize the five-shilling piece has failed, failed ignominiously, and failed deservedly. Half-a-crown is a lovable coin, but a whole crown is a detestable contrivance. Let Mr. Winterton think this over very carefully before he again lashes out against half-and-half things. Let him have a good look at every half-crown that comes into his possession. If he looks at it, he will fall in love with it; and if he has once become fond of it, he will attack it no more. He will probably go to the other extreme and preach a sermon in defence of it. I shall stroll into St. Mark's some fine evening; and Mr. Winterton will announce as his text the wise man's prayer: 'Give me neither poverty nor riches; feed me with food convenient for me,' and he will preach an eloquent sermon on moderation. He will point out that there are innumerable half-and-half things that are much more admirable than things more decided and pronounced. Are not spring and autumn—the betwixt and between seasons—at least as beautiful as either midwinter or midsummer? And certainly any pair of lovers would tell Mr. Winterton that the dusk, the twilight, and the gloaming are infinitely more delicious than either the glare of midday or the blackness of midnight.

I knew a man in New Zealand who, through no fault of his own, lost every penny that he owned. The loss fell upon him in the heat and burden of life's day. His domestic responsibilities were at their heaviest, and it looked very unlikely that he would be able to retrieve his fallen fortunes. Then came years of grim and desperate struggle, out of which he finally emerged triumphantly. But he afterwards told me that the great and memorable hour in that tremendous fight with fate was not the day on which his friends congratulated him on his success, but the day on which he himself saw that his task would be achieved. There were no applauding voices. To every eye but his that day was exactly like the day before. But it was on that day that it came to him that he had broken the back of his undertaking. He had turned the corner. It was not yet summer-time; but the winter was past and gone. The flowers were not yet blooming, and the birds were not yet singing; yet that day brought to him a joy greater than any that he knew in the after-days when he again found himself revelling in an established prosperity.

In that new sermon that I hope to hear him preach Mr. Winterton will belaud many of those half-and-half things that, in his earlier diatribe, he so roundly denounced. There is room for just such a sermon, a sermon in praise of mediocrity. Dr. Oliver Wendell Holmes divided men into two classes. There are, he said, men of the cat class and men of the squirrel class. A squirrel is, for awhile, an engaging companion. It is full of life, overflowing with exuberance and vitality; it is nimble, brisk, and sprightly, leaping over everything and climbing everywhere ; it is full of surprises, and astonishes you every second by its agility and its curious antics. But it soon tires you, and you are glad to see it safely restored to its cage. Similarly, according to the 'Autocrat,' there are people with nimble minds. They are lively, jerky, and smart. Their thoughts do not run in the natural order of sequence. They say bright things on all possible subjects, but their zigzags rack you to death. 'After a jolting half-hour with one of these jerky companions, talking with a dull friend affords great relief. It is like taking the cat in your lap after holding a squirrel. A ground-glass shade over a gas-lamp does not bring more solace to our dazzled eyes than such a one to our minds.' Again and again in the course of his breakfast-table conversations the 'Autocrat' takes occasion to express his appreciation of the services rendered to their kind by people who are by no means brilliant.

This reminds me of Walter Bagehot. I doubt very much whether Bagehot ever saw the 'Autocrat.' But he would certainly have argued that for the ideal specimen of the cat class of men you have only to look at the average Englishman, whilst for the ideal specimen of the squirrel class you have but to visit France. 'I need not say,' he writes, 'that in real sound stupidity the English are unrivalled You will hear more wit, and better wit, in an Irish street row than would keep the British Parliament in humour for five weeks. Whom so soporific as the average Englishman? His talk is of crops and bullocks; his head replete with rustic visions of mutton and turnips. Notwithstanding, he is the salt of the earth. The world holds nothing worthy to be compared with him.' Against all this Bagehot sets your vivacious but evanescent Frenchman, but he cuts a poor figure in the contrast. The pity of it is, exclaims Bagehot, that a Frenchman cannot be dull. He belongs essentially to the squirrel class. He is gay, vivacious, full of animation. Dullness is to him the sin unpardonable. He hates nothing so much as ennui; he dreads becoming *blasé*. Every phase of life must glitter and sparkle, or it bores him beyond endurance. But you have only to glance at a map of the world to see which is the more successful—catdom or squirreldom. Bagehot maintains that the Frenchman is too clever by half. By half, mark you! Let Mr. Winterton make a note of that. He will find it very useful when he is preparing his new sermon in praise of half-and-half things. Obviously, the person who aims at perpetual brilliance must leave undone many commonplace things that are really well worth doing, and must say and do many smart things that can compass no practical end. Mr. Winterton will be surprised at discovering how much there is to be said in praise of just ordinary people. He will fall in love with mediocrity. He will grow as fond as I am of half-crowns.

I do not know how Mr. Winterton will bring his new sermon to a close. Perhaps Cowper's Cottager will furnish him with a fitting climax:

> Yon cottager who weaves at her own door,
> Pillow and bobbins all her little store,
> Content though mean, and cheerful, if not gay,
> Shuffling her threads about the livelong day,
> Just earns a scanty pittance, and at night
> Lies down secure, her heart and pocket light;
> She for her humble sphere by nature fit,
> Has little understanding and no wit,
> Receives no praise, but (though her lot be such,
> Toilsome and indigent), she renders much;
> Just knows, and knows no more, her Bible true,
> A truth the brilliant Frenchman never knew,
> And in that charter reads with sparkling eyes
> Her title to a treasure in the skies.

The notable thing about this good lady, be it observed, is her mediocrity. She is neither ignorant nor scholarly; neither very rich nor very poor; neither gloomy nor gay. She must be ranked among the half-and-half things. And ranked with those half-and-half things, she is in excellent company. For she is in the company of the spring and the autumn, the dawn and the twilight, the girl at the hospital gates, Mr. Pomey's 'Convalescent'—and my half-crowns.

PART III

I

EARTHQUAKES

HAVE I ever written on earthquakes, weddings, sermons, and similar volcanic disturbances? I think not; and will therefore endeavour to repair the omission. In my old New Zealand days I used to indulge in porridge regularly and earthquakes occasionally—although the order seemed now and again in danger of getting reversed. I remember, soon after my arrival at Mosgiel, going to stay at a farm on the top of the hill—a farm that is already familiar to my earlier readers as the home of 'Granny.' On retiring the first night, I was told that the family breakfasted early, but that I was to lie still until I was called. Being very tired, I consented without violent demur, and was soon lost to all the world. I was awakened, however, by a loud noise. It seemed to me that somebody was not only banging at the door, but endeavouring to wrench it from its hinges. I sprang up, struck a match, and consulted my watch. It was just five o'clock. 'If this,' I said to myself, 'is the indulgence allowed to guests, at what weird hour, I wonder, does the family take breakfast?' There was no time, however, for nice mathematical computations of that sort. I hastily dressed and hurried out into the great farm kitchen. The daughter of the home stared at me as if she had confronted a ghost. I apologized for having put her to the trouble of calling me. 'Calling you!' she exclaimed. 'Why, nobody called you! The boys are not up yet!' I described the din that had scared me from my bed. 'Oh,' she replied, her face suddenly illumined, 'that was just the earthquake!' I resolved that never again would I be victimized by a practical joke of that kind.

After that I had worse experiences, but they were less humiliating. At dead of night I left my unsteady bed and, looking out of the window, found the birds flying around the swaying trees and the cattle tearing about the shuddering fields—all in the wildest confusion and dismay. But the antics soon ceased. The earth grew still; the starlings returned to their nests among the firs; the terrified cattle became calm; and I stole back to bed. Again, in November, 1901, on the occasion of the famous Cheviot earthquake, I happened to be staying within the zone of disturbance. How vividly I recall the groaning of the doors and the cracking of the windows! I was standing in my room at the moment, and I remember sitting abruptly down in order to save Nature the trouble, in the course of her frolic, of reducing me compulsorily to horizontality. It may not have been dignified; but, when tricks are being played, it is usually best to enter cheerfully into the spirit of the thing.

Now we happen to be living on a world in which earthquakes are the fashion. On the average there is an earthquake every quarter of an hour. About thirty or forty thousand occur annually. Every few minutes the earth shakes itself, like a dog coming out of the water; and, like the dog, the earth seems to feel all the better for the convulsion. The globe on which we live, for all her stolid appearance, is a nervy creature and has a creepy skin. She is all twitches.

Earthquakes are good things. How do I know? In two ways. First of all, they happen; and is it thinkable that the earth would quake every few minutes, year in and year out, unless earthquakes were good for her health? And then, too, the great geologists say as much, and thus philosophy is fortified by science. You never hear of an earthquake in a desert. Perhaps, if you did, the desert would remain a desert no longer. What is it that Macaulay says in his essay on 'The Principal

Italian Writers'? 'As the richest vineyards and the sweetest flowers always grow on the soil which has been fertilized by the fiery deluge of a volcano, so the finest works of the imagination have always been produced in time of political convulsion.' A farm is nothing without a plough. The earth needs to be torn up every now and again. That is why we have earthquakes.

The best description of an earthquake is Robinson Crusoe's. But, unhappily, Crusoe was too frightened, when he felt his island rocking to and fro, to hear what the earthquake had to say for itself. Had Crusoe listened, this is what the earthquake would have said to him: 'Think yourself lucky, O Robinson Crusoe,' it would have observed, 'that you were building a hut and not a palace. We earthquakes come to teach the world simplicity. If men live in hair tents or wooden cabins, we earthquakes never hurt them. But if they live in castles or palaces, we bury them in the wreckage of their splendour!' If I remember rightly, Gibbon has something to the same effect. In describing the loss of Berytus by volcanic disturbance he remarks that, in the day when the earth reels, the architect becomes the enemy of mankind. The hut of the savage or the tent of the Arab may be thrown down without injury to the inhabitant; but the rich marbles of the patrician are dashed on his own head and an entire people is buried beneath the ruins of their stately architecture. Did not the Incas of Peru deride the folly of the Spaniards who, with so much cost and labour, erected their own sepulchres? An earthquake gives a savage cause to laugh at civilization.

But there is more in it than this. Robinson Crusoe first began to think seriously about eternal things when he found his island rocking beneath his feet. An earthquake is an eloquent preacher. It sets a man wondering if he ought to build all his hopes on a thing that shakes and reels and twitches. Ought he not, to use Victor Hugo's simile, ought he not to be

> . . . like the bird
> Who, pausing in her flight
> Awhile on boughs too light,
> Feels them give way beneath her, and yet sings,
> Knowing that she hath wings?

But this screed of mine has already received its baptism of fire. It has run the gauntlet of criticism. Even before the last sheets have been written, the first sheets have been read. And my severest, yet most appreciative, critic demands an explanation of my very first sentence.

'What on earth do you mean,' she asks, 'by grouping "*earthquakes, weddings, sermons, and similar volcanic disturbances*" under a common heading? What has an earthquake to do with a wedding? And what has either of them to do with a sermon?'

I am afraid that on this occasion my grand chief critic is exhibiting something less than her usual insight and perspicacity, for, surely, the connexion between these things is sufficiently clear! If a wedding is not an earthquake, what is it? If a sermon is not a volcanic eruption, what can you call it? I am really surprised that there should be any dubiety on that point.

To prove that a wedding is an earthquake, and a good one, I shall have to call a pair of witnesses—a lady and a gentleman. And by the time I have done with them I confidently anticipate that all the ladies and gentlemen who know anything about it will clamour for permission to give corroborative evidence. The witnesses whom I have decided to subpoena are Miss Rosaline Masson and Mr. A. C. Benson.

Whilst Miss Masson is getting her breath we will take the testimony of Mr. Benson. Mr. Benson, as everybody knows, is the son of an Archbishop, and is himself a schoolmaster and a brilliant essayist. A few years ago Mr. Benson gave us a characteristic essay entitled 'The Search.' Mr. Benson tells how he had been spending an evening with a rich and elderly bachelor. They had dined 'with that kind of simplicity that can only be attained by wealth' at this gentleman's finely appointed house in London. Then they settled down to talk. Mr. Benson asked why his friend, possessing so much, worked so hard. The reply was startling. He worked so hard because it did not suit him to be unoccupied—to think! 'And then he suddenly said, with great seriousness, that he felt rather bitterly, now that life was nearly over, that he had somehow lost his way, and that he had always been bustling about on the outskirts of life. He went on to say that the mischief had been that he had never married. "What I feel that I want now," he said, "is the kind of unavoidable duty which comes from having people whose lives are really bound up with one's own. To put it at the worst, if I had a fretful, invalid wife and some ill-conditioned, ungainly children, *that* would be at all events a reality. I should have people to consider, to conciliate, to defend, to help, to keep on good terms with, to make the best of—and I hope, too, that some love would come in somewhere! But——"' That is all. But is it not very much? It means that there had been no eruption, no earthquake. The depths had never been broken up. As I said just now, you never hear of an earthquake in a desert; if you did, it would be a desert no longer. That was precisely the tragedy of Mr. Benson's friend. Was I so very far astray when I included earthquakes and weddings under a common heading?

But I must apologize to Miss Masson for having kept her waiting so long. Miss Masson has given us a lovely little monograph on Wordsworth. But on the last page she confesses that Wordsworth lacked a certain indefinable something. He could sing, as nobody else has ever sung, of skylarks and linnets, of redbreasts and butterflies, of daisies and daffodils. But, after all, life does not consist of daisies and daffodils. Wordsworth lacked something; what was it, and why was it? The secret is, Miss Masson declares, that in his own life the poet suffered no overwhelming experience of personal passion; there was no tremendousness in him; he never trailed his clouds of glory through the fire. Wordsworth never experienced an earthquake.

At a concert one evening I heard a beautiful girl sing a beautiful song. And yet when the last rich note trembled away into silence, I had a vague feeling of discontent. I missed something, I knew not what. I confessed this to a friend on the way home. 'Yes,' he replied, 'I noticed it. Some day her heart will be broken, and after that she will sing the song again; and then, if you hear her, you will be satisfied!' It was the earthquake that was wanting.

'Rock of Ages, cleft for me'—
  Thoughtlessly the maiden sung;
Fell the words unconsciously
  From her girlish, gleeful tongue;

Sang as little children sing,
  Sang as sing the birds in June,
Fell the words like light leaves down
  On the current of the tune—
'Rock of Ages, cleft for me,
  Let me hide myself in Thee.'

'Rock of Ages, cleft for me'—
  'Twas a woman sang them now,
Pleadingly and prayerfully—
  Every word her heart did know.
Rose the song as storm-tossed bird
  Beats with weary wing the air,
Every note with sorrow stirred,
  Every syllable a prayer—
'Rock of Ages, cleft for me,
  Let me hide myself in Thee.'

But I shall be reminded that I included sermons in that opening sentence of mine. And what of that? The sermon that is not a volcanic eruption is not worth hearing. 'I once heard a preacher,' Emerson tells us, 'who sorely tempted me to say that I would go to church no more. Men go, thought I, where they are wont to go, else had no soul entered the temple that morning. A snowstorm was falling around. The snowstorm was real; the preacher was merely spectral, and the eye felt the sad contrast in looking at him and then out from the window behind him into the beautiful meteor of the snow. He had lived in vain. He uttered no word intimating that he had laughed or wept, was married or in love, had been commended or cheated or chagrined.'

It is not pleasant to think of poor Emerson sitting in the cold church that wintry morning, longing for some warm word from a human heart and having to go out into the snowstorm disappointed. And it is still more painful to reflect that the whole congregation that bleak morning, like Milton's 'hungry sheep, looked up and were not fed.' What a pity that the spirit of the preacher had never been swept by some wild volcanic fires! What a pity that his heart had never been shattered! What a pity that the depths of the good man's soul had never been broken up! In contrast with Emerson's pitiful experience, let me tell another story:

God sent six children to the Manse,
 And one was crooked and strange,
And often through the hushed, sad house
 Half-frenziedly would range.

And none in such dark time had skill
 To calm that spirit wild—
None but the grave, strong minister,
 Who fondly loved the child.

And so through many a weary night
 He sat and talked and sang,
And soothed the lad the while his heart
 Was torn with many a pang.

Then, when, with calm face vigil-pale,
 He stood before his flock,
And great truths from his struck heart poured
 Like streams from Moses' rock.

And every hearer owned his grace,
  And tears wet every cheek,
From pew to pew the whisper went—
  'His lad's been bad this week.'

Cold-blooded critics may censure me if they will for having linked earthquakes with sermons; but no minister who knows the rapture of his calling will doubt for one moment the essential relationship. He knows that the only religion that has ever moved profoundly the lives of men is the religion of a divine heart that was broken for the healing of the world.

II

THE KING'S JESTER

I HAVE often wondered if we gained much by abolishing the fool—I mean, of course, the professional fool—from courts, castles, and a few other places. It is at least arguable that it would have been better, instead of banishing the fool from the large houses to have introduced him into the small ones. If a thing is a good thing, why should not everybody enjoy it? And a fool is a good thing! Look at the history-books! Look at Wamba in *Ivanhoe!* There is no gainsaying the fact that the fool cuts a striking and impressive figure in the brave pageant of mediaeval story. I suspect that at some time or other we have all felt a sneaking admiration for him. There he is, with his variegated costume, his flying coat-tails, his pointed slippers, his ass's ears, his cap and bells, and all the rest of it. No royal palace or baronial hall was complete without its jester.

And, depend upon it, it was some true human instinct that placed him there. Review these odd characters for a moment in grotesque but picturesque procession! And from Touchstone, the prince of Shakespearian clowns, to Archie Armstrong, the last of our Court Jesters, they make up an amiable and inviting company. Taking them as a whole, they are a lovable lot. Dickens touched with the wand of his genius the apparently sordid assemblage known as Sleary's Circus Troupe. Instantly an atmosphere of pathos and romance enveloped the performers; and we have all felt tenderly towards smirking clowns and tinselled equestriennes ever since. If only the same wizard had taken it into his head to write a story of the Middle Ages, I am certain that he would have flung the same resistless glamour over the person of the Court Jester. We should all have fallen in love with him; it is even possible that we should have wanted to popularize him. The fool was a fool, it is true; but, generally speaking, the folly of that fool was a little in advance of ordinary people's wisdom. 'He is undoubtedly crackt,' says Miss Baillie in the course of her criticism of poor Touchstone, 'but, then, the very cracks in his brain are chinks which let in the light.' Taking Miss Baillie's criticism at face value, it suggests a curious question. Is it not worth while having a few cracks in your brain if through those chinks the light comes streaming? And if there are a few men in the world whose brains, like those of Touchstone, admit the light, ought they to be banished from courts and castles? Ought they not rather to be welcomed everywhere?

But I ought to proceed no farther until I have explained the circumstances that led me to break into this strain. Yesterday afternoon I was lying on a grassy cliff overlooking the sea. To my left, down the slope, was a cluster of picturesque old fisher-huts. Far below me the waves were playing over an enormous reef. As I looked down I could see a score of people, shoeless and stockingless, clambering over the rocks in search of such mysterious treasure as the sea had deposited among the cracks and crevices. But I had the laugh of all of them. For I lay still upon the grass and found treasure that put their shells and seaweed to shame. I was reading *The Poet at the Breakfast-table* when I came upon this gem. *'One does not have to be a king,'* says the Poet, *'to know what it is to keep a king's jester.'* What does he mean? It is a case of *'Sez I to myself, says I.'* The Old Master is thinking of that inner voice that sometimes speaks in the depths of a man's soul; and he has been telling of some of the brutally candid criticisms that this second self occasionally addresses to the primary self. 'I never got such abuse from any blackguard in my life as I get from that

Number Two of me! *One does not have to be a king to know what it is to keep a king's jester.'*

The point clearly is that, both amidst the dazzling splendours of the court and amidst the awful solitudes of the soul, the king's jester is the one man who can laugh at the king. And it is a fine thing for the king to have one man who will look into his face and laugh at him. It is a fine thing for us all to be laughed at at times. That is why I am inclined to lament the abolition of fools. And that is why Jaques, in *As You Like It,* thought that to be a fool was to be the finest creature breathing. Cried he:

> A fool, a fool! I met a fool i' the forest,
> A motley fool! O, that I were a fool!
> I am ambitious for a motley coat!

The Duke, naturally enough, questions the melancholy Jaques as to why he is so eager for a fool's cap. And Jaques replies that he would fain be a fool because a fool can speak the truth, fearing the face of no man.

> . . . I must have liberty
> Withal, as large a charter as the wind,
> To blow on whom I please . . .
> Invest me in my motley: give me leave
> To speak my mind, and I will through and through
> Cleanse the foul body of th' infected world
> If they will patiently receive my medicine.

By this time, I flatter myself, the glory and dignity of the fool's profession is beginning to appear. Let us glance over the treasures we have picked up so far.

'It is a fine thing to be a fool,' says Joanna Baillie, 'for the cracks in a fool's brain are the chinks through which the light comes streaming.'

'It is a fine thing to be a fool,' says the melancholy Jaques, 'for a fool can speak the truth whenever he will, fearing the face of no man.'

'One does not have to be a king,' says the Poet of the Breakfast-table, 'to know what it is to keep a king's jester.'

That is the beauty of it. I am not writing for kings. The number of kings who will read this essay of mine is, I am afraid, extremely limited. But kings are not the only people in the world who need to be told the truth. Kings are not the only people in the world who deserve to be laughed at. They were wise kings who taught their jesters to laugh them out of their follies. And if I am half as wise as I sometimes pretend to be, I shall encourage my other self, my Number Two, my Court Jester, to lift up his voice in loud guffaw and boisterous cachinnation at my expense. In his lectures on *Conscience,* Dr. Joseph Cook has a notable address on 'The Laughter of the Soul at Itself.' Almost the whole of the lecture is occupied with one illustration—the story of Jean Valjean. Those who have read Victor Hugo's masterpiece—in some respects the greatest novel ever penned—will instantly see the relevance of the citation. They will recall the skill with which Hugo piles up the interest of the great story until the climax is reached. And at that terrific climax Jean Valjean has to make his great decision. In reality he is an escaped convict; but he is living under an assumed name, is doing well, is the owner of a vast industry, and is loved, honoured, and revered by all the townsfolk. But one day he reads that Jean Valjean has been recaptured and is before the court. Here, then, is the problem. Shall the real Jean Valjean dash to the ground his own happiness, and the happiness of thousands, by declaring himself? Or shall he maintain silence and allow the other man, who is known to be a rogue, to suffer in his stead? Jean Valjean sees, clear as noonday, what he *ought* to do. He knows that, strictly, he should 'follow right in scorn of consequence.' But he cannot bring himself to it. He resolves on silence and security. *'Just there,'* says Victor Hugo, *'just there he heard an internal burst of laughter!'* It was the laughter of the soul at itself. Jean Valjean was no king; he was a convict; but, as the Poet of the Breakfast-table says, he knew what it was to keep a king's jester.

I am surprised that Dr. Joseph Cook, an American lecturing to Americans, should have gone to French literature for his illustration, excellent as that illustration is. For he might have found an equally good one by staying at home. Nathaniel Hawthorne was also an American; and the laughter even of Jean Valjean is less pronounced than the terrible laughter of Arthur Dimmesdale. Arthur Dimmesdale was a minister; and he and Hester Prynne had sinned. She bore every day the burning brand of her shame, but no inquisitor could wring from her the name of her partner in guilt. Like Jean Valjean, the Reverend Arthur Dimmesdale had to make a great decision. Should he confess his iniquity and stand in that New England pillory by the side of Hester Prynne? Or should he keep his frightful secret locked up in his own breast and let Hester bear the shame alone? He thought of his name, his position, his influence, his crowded congregation; and he kept silence. He kept silence, that is to say, so far as the world knew. But within! Walking along the streets of his parish, he fancied that he saw himself standing in the pillory beside Hester Prynne, whilst around him there stood, gaping up at him in horror-stricken bewilderment, the officers of the church, the august personages who came from the best dwellings in the city to listen to his eloquence, the decorous matrons who presided over the elegant households in his great congregation, and 'the young virgins who idolized their minister and had made a shrine for him in their white bosoms.' And as the horror of this picture burst upon his fancy, there rose, in the soul of the distracted young minister, 'a great peal of laughter.' Later on Hester tries, good soul that she is, to comfort him.

'The people reverence thee,' she says. 'And surely thou workest good among them! Doth this bring thee no comfort?'

'Misery, Hester, more and more misery! What can a ruined soul like mine effect towards the redemption of other souls? Or a polluted soul towards their purification? Canst thou deem it a consolation that I must stand up in my pulpit, must meet so many eyes turned toward my face as if the light of heaven were beaming from it, must see my flock listening to my words as if a tongue of Pentecost were speaking, and then look inward and discern the black reality! I have laughed, in bitterness and agony of heart, at the contrast between what I *seem* and what I *am!* And Satan laughs at it!'

Arthur Dimmesdale was no king; but he knew what it was to keep a king's jester. And, even in the pulpit, his Court Jester looked him full in the face and laughed at him! It was the laughter of the soul at itself—the most terrible laughter of all. And his Court Jester gave him no rest day or night until he threw aside all seeming and made his great confession. And then, but not till then, the Court Jester bowed respectfully to his lord, and retired.

Yes, it does us all good to be laughed at. I sometimes wish that a visitor from Mars would light on this planet just to laugh at us. He would see the funny side of things as we, the inhabitants of the sphere, can never hope to do. He would go to our public libraries, expecting to find them crowded with ignorant people hungry for knowledge. He would find them the haunts of bookworms and philosophers! He would go to our banks, expecting to find them stormed by those who, lacking wealth, had come to fill their hands with treasure. He would find them thronged with the wealthy and the prosperous! He would go to our great banquets, expecting to find the seats filled with the ragged and the starving. He would find them occupied by the sleek, the well-fed, the well-to-do! He would come to our churches, expecting that in a world that had received a special revelation of divine regard all the sinners on the face of the earth would rush to hear the message of redeeming love; but he would be sadly disillusioned! And he would laugh! Oh, how he would laugh at the madness of our topsyturvy world! His laughter would shake the globe from pole to pole and be heard, like distant thunder, in his native sphere. And that reverberating peal would do us all good. We should have a wiser world if some clear-sighted fool from the celestial spaces were sometimes to come and laugh at us.

The world has never been particularly clever in recognizing its fools. We so often play charades and indulge in make-believe. It does not at all follow, because a man wears a crown, that he is therefore kingly. It does not at all follow, because a man wears a cap and bells, that he is therefore mad. It often happened, in those archaic days when courts and castles kept their fools, that the fool was the only wise man on the premises. Wisdom often masquerades. She does not cry, nor lift up, nor cause her voice to be heard in the street. As Joaquin Miller says:

> Ah, there be souls none understand,
> Like clouds, they cannot touch the land,
> Drive as they may by field or town.
> Then we look wise at this, and frown,
> And we cry, 'Fool!' and cry, 'Take hold
> Of earth, and fashion gods of gold!'
>
> Unanchored ships, that blow and blow,
> Sail to and fro, and then go down
> In unknown seas that none shall know,
> Without one ripple of renown;
> Poor drifting dreamers, sailing by,
> That seem to only live to die.

Call these not fools; the test of worth
Is not the hold you have on earth.
Lo, there be gentlest souls, sea blown,
That know not any harbour known;
And it may be the reason is
They touch on fairer shores than this.

To be a fool—so thought the melancholy Jaques—was to be the finest creature breathing!

A fool, a fool! I met a fool i' the forest,
A motley fool! O, that I were a fool!
I am ambitious for a motley coat!

I find that the good Jaques is not alone. Dr. Alexander Whyte, in his Lecture on Festus, quotes old Matthew Mead as saying that 'he is no true Christian who is not the world's fool!' We shall get no farther than that!

'Oh, to be a fool!' sighs Miss Joanna Baillie, 'for the cracks in a fool's brain are the chinks through which the light comes streaming!'

'Oh, to be a fool!' cries the melancholy Jaques, 'for a fool can speak the truth whenever he will, fearing the face of no man!'

'Oh, to be a fool!' exclaims the Poet at the Breakfast-table, 'for a man has not to be a king to know what it is to keep a king's jester!'

'Oh, to be a fool!' prays old Matthew Mead, 'for he is no true Christian who is not the world's fool!'

Was I so very far astray when I suggested that we should have been wiser, instead of banishing fools from royal palaces and baronial halls, had we left them there, and introduced them into all our villas and cottages as well?

III

JOHN HAVELOCK'S ESCAPE

I

JOHN HAVELOCK was a giant by nature, a gentleman by instinct, a Christian by the grace of God, and a grocer by profession. I lay stress, at the very outset, upon this fourth dimension, because it is with John as a grocer that I am now principally concerned. John was a tremendous fellow. His huge form seems to tower up before me even as I write. I am not much short of six feet myself; but I felt a perfect pigmy when he was about. And he was usually about. For John was for twelve years one of my deacons, and no minister could have had a more staunch and faithful friend. When John first came to Mosgiel, he carried his entire stock-in-trade upon his big, broad back. Like a modern edition of Atlas bearing the earth upon his shoulders, John came over the hills supporting an enormous pack, beneath the weight of which even his titanic frame almost staggered. He hawked his groceries from door to door. People liked his pluck and admired his enterprise—he was scarcely more than a boy in those days. He rapidly built up a connexion. In a few months he was able to buy a pony and cart; then he opened a shop; and, within ten years, he owned the biggest store on the Taieri Plain. As a grocer, John was a phenomenal success; yet, oddly enough, John was not always content to be a grocer. During one brief phase of his eventful career he hankered after the ministry. And it is the story of his escape from such a catastrophe that I have set out to record.

II

Some men are made to be ministers; some are not made to be ministers; some are made *not* to be ministers. John Havelock belonged to this third class. He was as honest as the day, and his transparent honesty was the secret of his success as a grocer. But he was handicapped by defects that proclaimed to all who knew him his irremediable unfitness for the ministry. To begin with, he could not express himself. In ordinary conversation I have seen him waving his hands like signals of distress whilst he struggled vainly to think of the word he wanted. I have heard it said of some men that they speak as though they have swallowed a dictionary. John must certainly have swallowed his, for he could never find a word when he wanted it.

He would hum and ha, stutter and gesticulate, pull all kinds of grimaces, and express astonishment at the obstinacy of the elusive phrase ; but the truant word took no notice of his frantic behaviour ; it would never come.

Nor am I convinced that he possessed some of those deeper qualities that go to make up a really successful minister. He was too much of an idealist. He liked bad people, and would have laid down his life to save them. He liked good people, and would have gone to any trouble to serve them ; but that was about all. He never realized that he was living in a world in which very few people are altogether bad or altogether good. Most people are half and half, and it is a minister's business to take people as he finds them and make the best he can of them. John could never do that. Had he become a minister, and had one member of his flock gone astray, John would have been like the good shepherd of the Gospels. He would have left everything, and would have gone out into the wilderness, and would have searched for that which was lost until he found it. And, when he had found it, he would have brought it back to the fold rejoicing. Such an experience would have been like a foretaste of heaven to John. And then again he would have revelled in the company of good people. But no very great proportion of a minister's life is spent either with the sheep that go hopelessly astray or with the sheep that remain demurely in the fold. Each of the ninety and nine sheep which go not astray has some little sheepish obstinacies that have to be watched, and some little sheepish stupidities that have to be endured, and some little sheepish peculiarities that have to be studied; and John would have been all at sea in this realm of things. He loved bad men and good men, but he had no patience with anything betwixt and between. He was an idealist. In some ways he was too good to make a successful minister.

III

John often told me the story of his escape. He always told it to the accompaniment of a storm of laughter; but you could feel that tears were not far away. The lure of the pulpit arose very largely from John's unbounded admiration of the minister of his boyhood, the Rev. Alfred South. He regarded his old minister as the incarnation of all human nobleness; and the excellence of the man threw a new lustre, in John's eyes, about his sacred calling. To be a minister seemed to John the very climax of human greatness, the loftiest altitude of moral grandeur. The very thought of it captivated his whole fancy. It haunted his waking imaginations and wove itself into his night-time dreams. The idea was a for long time purely impersonal. He did not connect himself with it in any way. It was just the abstract thought of being a minister, the sublimity of being a minister! But at length he found his own face creeping into the vision. At first he dismissed the thought with horror. He drove it away impatiently, as he would have brushed away a fly that threatened to settle on a sacred and beautiful picture. But it came back again and again in spite of him. At last his own face became part of the vision. He could not exclude it. And then he asked himself if he *ought* any longer to try to exclude it? Might not this be to him a solemn and imperative call? *This* was the struggle that was proceeding in his soul whilst his body was aching under the burden of the great pack that he bore so bravely over the hills. John had a conscience as tender as a baby's finger-tips. Climbing a steep hill one day, he thought all the way up of Jonah. Jonah heard the call, and fled. John trembled lest he too should prove recreant to a divine commission. And all the way down the opposite slope, where the mountain range inclines to the plain below, he thought of Paul. 'I was not disobedient to the heavenly vision.' He came into the town and began selling his groceries. But every shilling seemed to burn his pockets. He felt that he had heard a higher voice and flouted it. He had been commanded to forsake all and follow like the disciples of old, and yet here he was, hugging his pack and making his profits still!

IV

A fortnight later the position became intolerable and a crisis was precipitated. John could not sleep at night; he tossed to and fro in a fever of uncertainty and cruel doubt. And all day long his mind was focused upon his inner struggle rather than upon his groceries. He made mistakes; gave customers goods for which they had not asked, and returned them too much change. Twice in one day he was charged with being in love. He could not truthfully deny the soft impeachment, for it was perfectly true; and his affection for Kit only increased his anxiety to make no false step. She was a wise little woman. The prospect of being the mistress of a manse was as sweet to her as John's radiant dreams of the ministry were to him. But love had not blinded her eyes to his defects. She would rather see him a successful merchant and an honoured citizen than see him a failure in the ministry. She, therefore, feigned indifference concerning the change at which he hinted, but spoke proudly of his present success in business, and of the good they would be able to do if, some day, fortune came their way. Yes, John was in love; but Kit was not to blame for the blunders that he made that day.

That night when John reached home, sick at heart and tired out, a letter awaited him. It was from the secretary of the church, asking him to conduct a cottage prayer-meeting at a certain home on the following Thursday evening. John seized a pen; scribbled off a reply, agreeing to conduct the service; and went out to post it. It was a lovely night, mild and starlit. It was late, and there was not a soul about. John had not troubled to put on his hat, and he felt soothed by the cool breeze as it played caressingly with his hair. Suddenly, on the way back from the post, a strange impulse took possession of him. He lifted the panel and let himself into a field at the far end of which some cattle were huddled together. He threw himself on his knees on the grass and, turning his face to the skies, he prayed. 'O Lord,' he exclaimed passionately, 'wouldst Thou have me to be Thy minister? Show me Thy way, O Lord! If it be Thy will that I should take this step, grant me some token of Thy favour as I preach Thy Word on Thursday! Let it be seen that God is with me and that I do but speak in His holy name! And if *not*, O Lord——! If it be *not* Thy will that I should be one of Thy ministers, then, I entreat Thee, put me to confusion before all who shall attend! Let it be seen that Thou hast not called me! Pity Thy servant in his distress and vouchsafe to him the sign that he desires!' John rose; some cool raindrops fell refreshingly upon his flushed face; he hurried home, threw himself into bed, and slept like a top.

V

'I shall never forget that Thursday night as long as I live,' John often said to me. 'I was determined that, if things went wrong, they should go wrong through no neglect of mine. I chose my text on the Sunday and spent every scrap of spare time preparing my address. I went over it again and again in the course of my rounds. I selected the hymns and practised them most carefully with the lady who was to play the organ. I even arranged with the two men who were to lead us in prayer. I never made such careful preparation for a meeting in my life. Had I been commanded to preach before the King I could not have attended more punctiliously to every detail. Half an hour before the time, I walked down to the house at which the meeting was to be held, and saw to it that the chairs, the table, the lights, and everything else were to my liking. Just after I had taken my place in the arm-chair at the table, Kit entered with her mother and smiled meaningly and sympathetically.

'At eight o'clock the big room was comfortably

filled, and I started to the tick. It seemed as though nothing could go wrong. The singing was hearty; the prayers were models of reverence and fervour; I read the Scripture amidst a silence that showed that no single listener was willing to miss one precious syllable of the sublime message. The extreme nervousness that had victimized me all day passed from me like a cloud, and I experienced a confidence and self-possession I had rarely known before. At length I announced the hymn that immediately preceded my address. During the singing of the last verse I bowed my head and inwardly repeated the vow that I had uttered under the trees. The people resumed their seats; I rose.

'At that moment there was a commotion in the hall outside. A late-comer had arrived. It turned out to be a bustling little old lady of genial face and ample figure who lived just across the road. I paused, waiting for things to settle themselves. There was a shuffling of chairs. A man on the right-hand side of the door was about to place his chair for her when he saw that a man on the left-hand side of the door was offering his. Each started to move his chair, and each withdrew it on discovering the action of the other. The old lady took it for granted that her chair was now in place and sat down! There was a thud; a score of piercing screams; and then, when it was clear that the good body was none the worse for her prostration, a general burst of laughter. The old lady rose and scolded first the man on the right and then the man on the left; there were apologies and explanations; the company compared notes as to what each saw and heard and thought. There was more laughter after each narration, and the possibilities of restoring solemnity and resuming the meeting vanished into thin air. The carefully prepared address was never delivered; the prayer under the trees had been answered. When I said 'Good-night' to them all, they were laughing good-naturedly. On Kit's face I saw a look of wistful sadness. Kit saw the tragedy that underlay the comedy. Kit understood.'

VI

John assures me that he went home that night feeling neither discomfited nor ashamed. The issues to him were so momentous that the embarrassment of the situation did not affect him. The other afternoon I saw a naval signalman waving flags to a battleship out at sea. A little child was with me. He thought the flag-waving great fun. The officer on the battleship interpreted the message with grim seriousness. The people gathered that night saw things as my little boy saw the waving of the flags. To John the incident was pregnant with quite another significance. He was like the officer on the ship. He felt, he says, that a great load had been lifted from his shoulders. He threw himself into his business with a will. Nobody ever again accused him of being in love, although he and Kit were married the following year.

As I have said, he prospered phenomenally. Everything that he touched turned to gold. He made a fortune in no time. And it was just as well that he did. For, two years after his marriage, a baby-boy came to John's home. And, while the place was still ringing with his childish merriment, the little fellow went suddenly blind. Poor John and poor Kit! I was with them constantly in those days, and shall never forget their dumb but terrible anguish. Every morning they hurried to the bedside of their treasure, hoping against hope that the light had come back to Davie's eyes in the night. Then John made his great resolve. He determined to devote his life and his fortune to the service of his blind boy. Mosgiel was a small place, and there were no institutions there at which he could receive special training. John sold out; and went away to live in retirement near a large School for the Blind nearly a thousand miles away. He spent every moment of his time and every penny of his income in making a man of Davie. And again the most extraordinary success attended him. Davie became one of the most brilliant scholars and one of the most accomplished citizens that the Dominion of New Zealand ever produced.

The last time I saw John he was telling me proudly of Davie's triumphs. And then his mind harked back to the old days—the heavy pack, the golden dreams, and the never-to-be-forgotten prayer-meeting. 'I can see now,' he said, in a voice in which gratitude mingled with a certain indefinable sadness, 'I can see now that I should have cut a very poor figure in the ministry. And besides,' he added reflectively, 'I should never have been able to make a man of Davie. It was a great escape!' And Kit has often expressed the same sentiments in other words, although I have generally detected a moistening of the eye as she told the story.

IV

LONESOME GATE

LONESOME GATE, you must know, is in the Never-Never country. Right away up in the interior of Australia there were, years ago, two great sheep-runs adjoining each other: the Gallagher run and the Aberdeen run. A fence divided them, with gates across the roads. In course of time the Gallagher run came into the market, and was bought by the owner of the Aberdeen run. The necessity for fences and gates no longer existed. The fences were not removed, but were allowed to fall into disrepair. The consequence is that as you drive along the road from Wilbur's Creek to Tireni you come upon a great gate that stands there all by itself. You can scarcely see a trace of the fence in either direction. But there is the gate! And from the top bar the huge letters still shout as loudly as ever: *Please shut this gate!* One of these days it may occur to somebody to remove the obstruction; but meanwhile Lonesome Gate blocks the highway.

Now that the fences attached to it are gone, Lonesome Gate is a nuisance. No farmer jumps down from his gig to open it without wishing it at the bottom of the deep blue sea. Yet Lonesome Gate is not the only nuisance of its kind. Nobody can have knocked about the world very much without having come upon scores of such gates, standing all alone, with never a fence near them. And yet, obsessed with an exaggerated estimate of their own importance, they pathetically appeal to be kept shut! Things have a way of living too long.

Was there ever a finer movement than that which led to the establishment of the Pharisees? Foreign influences were surging into Palestine like a flood, and there was grave danger that the great Jewish tradition might be swept away before it. Then arose the Pharisees to keep alight the torch of patriotism in the Hebrew breast. It was a magnificent movement. But conditions changed. The Caesars conquered Palestine. A new atmosphere came into existence. For Pharisaism there was no longer room. But, like Lonesome Gate, which persists in surviving the fence that once stood beside it, Pharisaism refused to die. When it ceased to be beneficent it began to be baneful. And, as a consequence, the Pharisee stands in the New Testament as a thing of derision and contempt.

No; the gate is of no use after the fence attached

to it is gone. I can understand that, once in a blue moon, some bleary-eyed and dull-witted beast might come meandering down the road, find his progress arrested by the gate, and stand with his head over it until somebody should come and let him through. But that can only happen once in a blue moon. Ordinarily, all the cattle that come will see at a glance that the gate is a bogey; that there are no fences on either side of it; and that they can make headway against the barrier by the simple expedient of walking round it. I have no reason to suppose that Lonesome Gate is maintained by Government. But, without being too hard upon my political friends, I really should not be surprised if I were to hear from some one in the neighbourhood that, although the fences have vanished, the Government carefully repairs and repaints Lonesome Gate every year. Governments have a knack of doing that kind of thing. They erect gates against the cattle that stick blindly to the road; but they put up no fences against the creatures that will avoid the gate and go bellowing round it. They will legislate against noxious weeds and swine fever and riding on the footpath; but against the titanic evils that gnaw their way into a nation's heart and suck its very life-blood they will raise but few obstacles. They may maintain a gate, it is true, and may insist that that gate must be kept shut; but there is no fence, and the monstrous things rush in and trample down everything.

Then, again, at the opposite extreme, there is old John Cranston. John is a great temperance advocate. His enthusiasm, constantly at white heat, has always evoked my admiration; and his toil, always prodigious, has often shamed my own puny efforts in the same excellent cause. And yet, somehow, I thought of John Cranston as soon as I heard the story of Lonesome Gate. For I was never able to convince John Cranston that we need something beside the gate. I once invited him to church. He abruptly declined, and I fancied I detected a contemptuous curl on his lip. The churches, he said, were not practical enough for him. Religion was too other-worldly, too visionary, too nebulous. He thought that ministers should give up talking about some other world and do their best to patch up this one. I once asked him to support me in an effort I was making at that moment to minimize another glaring wrong. He rejected the proposal with disdain. What was the good, he wanted to know, of tinkering with this thing and that thing so long as the hotel bars were licensed to addle men's brains, degrade their characters, and ruin their homes? I assisted him by every means in my power in his heroic attempt to shut the drink evil out of the world. But he would never help me to bring the kingdom of God into it. He could never see that even a total abstainer might still be a fiend if, for example, he yielded to utter selfishness or was led captive of a vile temper. I had to give up reasoning with him. When I last saw him he was still working away at the gate. And I recognized that the gate was very necessary. But I often wished that his eyes could have been opened to see that the gate would be quite useless unless it were supported by stout fences on either side.

The real trouble lies in a lack of imagination. If those political and private individuals who are so enamoured of the gate that they never think about a fence would project their fancies into the mental processes of a flock of sheep, they would see at once the frailty of their reasoning. When Frank Buckland was revolutionizing the fisheries of England, he used to stand up to his waist in the English rivers and say to himself, 'Well, now, if I were a salmon, what would I do?' It would be a fine thing if these gate-worshippers would adopt similar tactics. Let them set out along the road from Tireni to Wilbur's Creek until they come to Lonesome Gate. Then let them stand in front of it for precisely sixty seconds, saying to themselves, 'Well, now, if I were some old bell-wether, leading a flock of sheep along this high-road, what would I do?' And at the expiration of the sixty seconds you will hear their peals of laughter though you be a mile away. What self-respecting bell-wether is going to be baulked by a gate, if the gate be unsupported by a fence or hedge? He will not even attempt to get through it or over it. He will go round it with all the flock thundering at his heels. If the road is blocked by a gate, why, the sheep will leave the road and take to the grass, that is all.

They will leave the road and take to the grass! That is the weakness of atheism, scepticism, agnosticism, and of all the denials and negations that ever were. The human mind moves naturally along the road of faith as the sheep move naturally along the road from Wilbur's Creek. Then its progress is abruptly challenged by some intellectual obstruction, as the progress of the sheep is challenged by Lonesome Gate. The highway of faith is blocked! A difficulty stands in the way! What will the mind do? It may attempt to get through or to get over for the sake of keeping to the road. But nine times out of ten the reason, baulked by the gate, takes to the grass. If it cannot pursue its course along the road of faith, it will defy the gate and forsake the highway at the same time. 'My lord,' said Beaconsfield, in addressing a famous gathering at Oxford 'my lord, man is a being born to believe; and if no Church comes forward with its title-deeds of truth, sustained by the traditions of sacred ages, and by the convictions of countless generations, to guide him, he will find altars and idols in his own heart and in his own imagination.' If, that is to say, the gate blocks his way, forbidding him to believe what he has been accustomed to believe, he will have his revenge by believing in spite of the gate ; but he will believe something much less believable. He will not be obstructed or turned back ; he will take to the grass.

In his *Old Red Sandstone*, Hugh Miller makes very merry at the expense of M. Maillet. 'This Maillet was much too great a philosopher to credit the scriptural account of Noah's flood ; yet he could believe that the whole family of birds had existed at one time as fishes, which, on being thrown ashore by the waves, had got feathers by accident ; and he could believe that men themselves are but the descendants of a tribe of sea monsters who, tiring of their proper element, crawled up the beach one sunny morning and, taking a fancy to the land, forgot to return !' Maillet came to the gate, and his advance along the highway of faith was blocked ; so he took to the grass. The faith lost him, it is true ; but the gate was cheated of its prey.

It has always been so. Show me an age in which a gate was set across the path of faith ; and I will show you an age in which, there being no fence, men set off across the grass. Man is by nature a believer ;

and, if you make it hard for him to believe the things that are best worth believing, he will still believe; but he will believe in the things that are least worth believing. In the days that followed the Restoration, when religion trudged barefoot and vice walked in golden slippers—the day of Hobbes and scepticism—men believed in ghosts as they had never done before. The churches were forsaken; but every lane had its spectre, and every street its haunted house! When, in the days of the Revolution, Frenchmen abjured Christianity, did they manage without a religion? Let Carlyle answer. 'Procureur Chaumette and Municipals and Departmentals arrive, and with them the strangest freightage—a New Religion! Demoiselle Candeille, of the opera, a woman fair to look on when well rouged; she, borne on palanquin shoulder high; with red woollen night-cap; in azure mantle; garlanded with oak; holding in her hand the Pike of the Jupiter-Peuple, sails in; heralded by white young women girt in tricolour. Let the world consider it! This, O National Convention, wonder of the universe, is our New Divinity!' What does it mean? It means that if the Revolutionists could not block faith altogether, they had a thousand times better have let it alone. They put up a gate across the main road; but there was no fence on either side; and the people, like a flock of sheep, turned from the road, but rushed on across the grass. They found themselves excluded from a religion that was sublime; so they concocted for themselves a religion that was ridiculous. 'Why, gentlemen,' said Napoleon, a few years later, 'it seems to me that you make up for believing nothing in the Bible by believing all the folly outside it!'

I remember once in New Zealand travelling in an express train with a gentleman who, growing confidential, opened his heart to me. He told me of his boyish experiences at church and Sunday school. He described to me his old home; his father's influence; and his mother's faith. He himself afterwards joined the church and taught in the Sunday school. Then he suddenly came upon the gate across the road. His Christian progress was challenged. A fellow clerk, for whom he entertained a kind of infatuation, had presented him with all the latest products of the cheap rationalistic press; and it had left his faith in fragments. I expressed my sympathy and sorrow.

'And so. now,' I added, 'you believe in nothing.'

'Oh, well,' he explained apologetically, 'I have joined a spiritualistic society, and am just now returning from a séance!'

The gate had not stopped him, for there was no fence. It had simply turned him from the path. He had taken to the grass. 'I have observed,' wrote James Russell Lowell, 'I have observed that many who deny the inspiration of Scripture hasten to redress the balance by giving a reverent credit to the revelations of inspired tables and camp-stools.'

That is always the trouble. The lover can bear with fortitude the rejection of his love; but it is a bitter thing for him to see the object of his strongest and tenderest affections in the embrace of one whom he knows to be altogether unworthy of her trust. It is sad enough to see men turn from the Church, from the Saviour, from the Cross; it is a thousand times sadder so see them, forsaking these things, become infatuated with frivolities and baubles. 'My people'—so runs one of the most affecting complaints of all time—'My people have committed two evils; they have forsaken Me, the Fountain of Living Waters, and have hewed out to themselves cisterns, broken cisterns, that can hold no water.' The worst of the fenceless gate on the road to the Celestial City is that, having no power to arrest the progress of the pilgrims, it forces them aside into those fields in which Giant Despair pounces upon them, and hurries them to his dismal dungeons.

V

SISTER KATHLEEN

This morning I pay my respects to the nurse. We meet often, and I am surprised that it has not occurred to me to make her the theme of an earlier contribution. In the hospital ward and in the sick-room the nurse and the minister exchange frequent courtesies; and if to the poor minister she sometimes seems a trifle imperious, he sets it down to her sense of the dignity and importance of her office, and secretly admires her all the more.

I can forgive any man for falling in love with a nurse. To tell the truth, I once fell in love with a nurse myself. But there were difficulties. To begin with, she was a devout and whole-souled Catholic, whilst I was a convinced young Protestant. That was serious. And then, to make matters worse, there was the minor circumstance that I was only fourteen, whilst she was over forty. Thus it came to pass that love's young dream was shattered; but to my dying day I shall never forget the face that, in hours of anguish and delirium, seemed to me like the face of an angel. Night and day, through weary weeks, she watched tirelessly beside me ; no vigil too long, and no trouble too great. I used to guess at what the doctors had said by closely scrutinizing her face. She would walk off with them when they left me. If she came back crooning to herself some jaunting little Irish melody, I knew that the doctors were satisfied. If she came back looking as though the weight of the world were on her shoulders, I knew that I was fighting an uphill battle ; and once, when things were very dark with me, I caught the glint of tears in her eyes. A few weeks later, when I was making headway rapidly, she would exchange meals with me. My bread-and-butter was cut and spread by machinery—each slice just like every other slice. Her bread was cut by hand ; the slices were irregular, and the butter was in neat little pats on the side of the plate. And each little delicacy that came her way she at once brought to me. We both cried when, the long, long struggle over at last, we said good-bye to each other. I have never since been able to look upon a nurse without blessing her ; and whenever I have been tempted to a too vigorous criticism of Roman Catholicism, I have been confronted by the imperishable memory of Sister Kathleen. She would have thought it heaven to lay down her life for her Church —or for her patients.

But, all such memories apart, he must have an adamantine soul who does not see something very attractive about a modern nurse. I say a modern nurse—for sufficient reasons. I am not praising Sarah Gamp. 'She was a fat old woman, this Mrs. Gamp, with a husky voice and a moist eye, which she had a remarkable power of turning up, and only showing the white of it. Her face—the nose in particular—was somewhat red and swollen, and it was difficult to enjoy her society without becoming conscious of a smell of spirits.' Her rusty black gown, rather the worse for snuff, and her huge umbrella have engaged the attention of ten thousand artists. She went to a lying-in or a laying-out with equal relish, being careful to adopt a beaming or lugubrious countenance according to the nature of the occasion. Mrs. Gamp has gone, and gone for good—in more senses than one. In her place we have a much more lovable figure. Never was transformation more complete. I was talking to a nurse half an hour ago. Her dainty costume, her immaculate apron and streamers, her faultless cuffs, collar, and cap are suggestive in themselves of that scrupulous cleanliness any violation of which is now regarded by science in the light of a crime. The cheerfulness of her face, the softness of her voice, the lightness of her tread, and the gentleness of her touch impart to the ward or the sick-room an atmosphere which would have been totally foreign to the ideas of Sarah Gamp. The musical jingle of the tiny implements that dangle from her waist, combined with her preternatural facility for laying her hand at a moment's notice on all kinds of mysterious appliances, are in themselves subtle reminders to the patient of a careful training and of a varied experience which, by inspiring confidence and restfulness, possess a healing virtue of their own. One does not care to imagine the uses to which Mrs. Gamp would have put a clinical thermometer ; nor dare I speculate as to what her reply would have been if a curious patient had ventured to ask her views on the general subject of bacteriology.

Nursing is neither a science nor an art ; it is something deeper and higher than either. It is an instinct, and a primal instinct at that. Drummond, in his *Ascent of Man,* implies that it is one of the highest of the primal instincts. I have sometimes wondered that the genial professor did not follow his great chapters on 'The Evolution of a Father' and 'The Evolution of a Mother' with a third on 'The Evolution of a Nurse.' For certainly the story of the coming of the modern nurse is one of the most romantic pieces of evolution that any thinker could record. Jack London, too, whose genius for portraying the inner side of animal life amounted almost to an intuition, commented repeatedly upon the marked propensity for nursing which some dogs exhibit. In *The Call of the Wild* he describes the misfortunes that overtook, and nearly killed, Buck, the great St. Bernard, on the long, exhausting trail. And he tells how Skeet, a little Irish setter, made friends with Buck, who, in a dying condition, was unable to resist her advances. 'She possessed,' the writer says, 'that doctor trait which some dogs have; and as a mother cat washes her kittens, so she washed and cleansed Buck's wounds. Regularly, each morning, she performed her self-appointed task, till he came to look for her ministrations as much as he did for his master's.' Any one who casually glances through a collection of stories illustrative of the sagacity of animals will find ample evidence of the existence of this curious phenomenon. In one way, it is even loftier than the maternal instinct, since it stands quite independently of the claim of kinship or any natural tie.

And so we climb these golden stairs. We follow the tortuous process of evolution up from the nest and the burrow and the lair. Tracing its upward course, we come at length upon Sarah Gamp. For we must be fair to Sarah Gamp. Let us admit that if, on the one hand, she has been put to shame by her gentler and more graceful successors, she was, on the other hand, herself an advance upon her remoter predecessors. Evolution moves upward and ever upward until we come to Florence Nightingale, to Sister Kathleen, and to the nurse whom I met at the hospital just now—the very incarnation of Longfellow's Evangeline:

> With light in her looks she entered the chambers of sickness,
> Noiselessly moved about the assiduous, careful attendants,
> Moistening the feverish lip and the aching brow, and in silence
> Closing the sightless eyes of the dead, and concealing their faces,
> Where on their pallets they lay, like drifts of snow by the roadside,
> Many a languid head, upraised as Evangeline entered,
> Turned on its pillow of pain to gaze while she passed; for her presence
> Fell on their hearts like a ray of the sun on the walls of a prison.

Mark Rutherford used to say that the modern nurse is about the strongest argument we have to prove that the world is not governed by the devil. 'Thank heaven,' he exclaims, 'that the modern hospital, with its sisters, gently nurtured, devoted to their duty with that pious earnestness which is a true religion, has supplied some evidences to prove that God rules His world!'

If this means anything, it means that the nurse represents in her own fair person one of the very finest triumphs of the Christian spirit in contact with mortal pain. She stands for one of the greatest strides in the whole history of human progress.

I like to watch her beautiful hands,
Slender, flexible, strong as steel—
In the rubber gloves that fit like skin—
At pitiful tasks that hurt to heal.

They move like Fate, those beautiful hands,
Firm, relentless—tender and kind.
Cleansing wounds at which others shrink,
Theirs is the strength that has love behind.

Merciless, merciful, beautiful hands—
Whether they bring relief or pain,
Those who have felt their healing touch
Will long, in need, for those hands again.

I am not surprised that in every city in Christendom efforts are being made to secure trained nurses for the poorest dwellers of the slums. Nor is it strange that in these vast Australias of ours, with their terrific solitudes, bush nursing schemes should be so popular. The world has few things of which it is entitled to be more proud than of the perfection to which the craft of nursing the sick has now been brought; and it is both natural and creditable that so strong a desire should be felt to extend the usefulness of this beneficent sisterhood to the lowest strata of society and to the loneliest outposts of civilization.

But deeper—let us go deeper! For see, whilst the patient recovers, the nurse tires! He gets stronger, but she grows weaker! Can it be that she is literally pouring the tides of her rich young life into his exhausted frame? 'That,' says the Autocrat of the Breakfast-table, 'is what makes her look so pale: she keeps the poor dying thing alive with her own blood. Ah!' he exclaims, 'illness is the real vampirism; think of living a year or two after one is dead, by sucking the life-blood out of a frail young creature at one's bedside! Well, souls grow white, as well as cheeks, in these holy duties; one that goes in a nurse, may come out an angel. God bless all good women! To their soft hands and pitying hearts we must all come at last!'

Two letters lie before me as I write. I do not need to search for the signature. I can tell by the handwriting that they come from the same person. Which things are an allegory, for, on a table near my desk, there stand a photograph of a nurse and a New Testament. I have not toilfully to trace the history of nursing on the one hand, nor to investigate the inspiration of the Scriptures on the other, in order to discover that the spirit of the nurse and the spirit of the New Testament were both breathed into them from the same divine source. In both I find the same sympathy with suffering, the same patience of pity, the same soft tenderness of touch. These, like the two letters, also reveal the same handwriting, and bear the same signature. As Charles P. Cleave so delicately sings:

I lay my hand on your aching brow,
Softly, so! And the pain grows still.
The moisture clings to my soothing palm
And you rest because I will.

You forget I am here? 'Tis the darkness hides.
I am always here, and your needs I know.
I tide you over the long, long night
To the shores of the morning glow.

So God's hand touches the aching soul;
Softly, so! And the pain He stills.
All the grief and woe from the soul He draws,
And we rest because He wills.

We forget—and yet He is always here!
He knows our needs and He heeds our sighs.
No night so long but He soothes and stills
Till the dawn-light rims the skies.

When one has drawn so awful, yet so apt, an analogy as this, there remains no more to be said. The case for the nurse is complete.

VI

OUR INTERRUPTIONS

INTERRUPTIONS are extremely vexatious; but, when all is said and done, it is by our interruptions that we reach our goals. I have the highest scientific authority for saying that it is the interruption that really matters. I am writing on the fiftieth anniversary of the invention of the cablegram; and the cablegram is the fruit of deliberate and systematic interruption. The story of Samuel Morse, the genius to whom we owe the introduction of our cablegrams, is a great religious romance. He was poor as poverty. Whilst he was puzzling out the details of his invention he was often compelled by sheer necessity to pass twenty-four hours without a meal. The suggestion of a submarine cable emanated largely from his homesickness. He was in Europe; his parents were in America; it took a month to send a letter. A sentence that he had once memorized at Yale haunted him night and day. It was: '*If the circuit of electricity be interrupted, the fluid will become visible; and, when it passes, it will leave an impression upon any intermediate body.'*

'If the circuit be interrupted! If the circuit be interrupted!' The words took complete possession of his brain. Morse found it impossible to resist the conclusion that if the interruption of the current must issue in visibility, it ought to be easy to turn the visibility into a code of signals. The visibility that resulted from the interruption of the current would, of course, take the form of a spark. 'Why not make that spark represent a part of speech, a letter, a number? Why not make the absence of the spark a part of speech; the duration of the absence a part? In short, why not have an alphabet, which should be the voice of electricity?' The idea reached its climax in his brain on a certain moonlight night on board the *Sully* as he was returning to America. He paced the deck all night, and by dawn the alphabet was complete. In his *History of the Telegraph in America,* Mr. Reid pays an eloquent tribute to the simplicity and perfection of that alphabet. 'Men can wink it with their eyes,' he says, 'they can beat it with their feet, and dying men have used it when vocal organs and the strength to write were exhausted. The prisoner can tap it on the wall or grating of his dungeon. Lovers in distant rooms can converse by it on the gas-pipe. Its uses are endless. It is the telegraphic language

of the world.' The tremendous and heroic struggle that eventually induced Parliaments and Congresses—always timid of sensational innovations—to finance Morse's project constitutes one of the great romances of commercial history. But it is pleasant to-day to remember that, after patiently enduring the withering scorn and pitiless ridicule that were everywhere heaped upon his startling idea of sending words along wires, he lived to see his invention become the most amazing financial triumph of his time. Moreover, he lived to wear the honours and decorations that all the Courts of Europe so plentifully thrust upon him. And all because he was the first to discover the value of an interruption!

How often it happens that a thing only becomes the more impressive and the more effective by being interrupted! Some of the loveliest things in life issue from our interruptions. Indeed, we begin life with an interruption. A woman finds that she must cancel all her engagements; and for a while we see her face no more. Then she reappears, with a baby in her arms. They say that some women evade marriage and motherhood just because it would involve life in such troublesome interruptions. It is difficult to believe that women can be so blind. The women whose lives have been interrupted in this way have discovered what Samuel Morse discovered fifty years ago, that an interruption may be the most fruitful and vital thing in history.

An interruption, like a rhetorical pause, emphasizes a thing. I recall several utterances that I must have forgotten long ago but for the fact that they were interrupted. Let me mention three. I remember being present, many years ago, at a great prayer-meeting in London. A little old gentleman in the body of the hall rose to lead us to the Throne of Grace. His voice was clear as a bell; his diction was reverent and beautiful; he prayed like a man inspired. But all at once his voice became tremulous with emotion, and a moment later it failed him altogether. For a few seconds there was an intense and painful stillness. Then the old gentleman strove bravely to resume his supplication. But after struggling with himself for a second or two, he shook his head sorrowfully. 'Take the meaning, Lord!' he managed to say, 'take the meaning!' and sat down. I am sure I should have forgotten the meeting, the graceful petitions, and the gentle pleader but for the affecting interruption. The interruption lifted it out of the commonplace and lent it a distinction.

The other evening I was conducting a very special Communion Service. To me the occasion was full of sacred significance, for it marked the anniversary of my ordination. An old minister was present, whose long record of distinguished service lent to his grey hairs an added glory. I had asked him to deliver a short pre-communion address. He spoke, with evident delight, of the exquisite completeness of his Lord's redemption; and, having poured out his heart to us, he took a step backward as though to resume his seat. But an afterthought seized him; he retraced that single step; and once more took his place at the desk. 'For sixty years,' he said, with manifest emotion, 'for sixty years I have served this Saviour, and do you think I have regretted it? Never once!' He resumed his seat, and I announced the next hymn, 'Rock of Ages, cleft for me'; and even as we sang

While I draw this fleeting breath,
When my eyelids close in death,
When I soar to realms unknown,
See Thee on Thy judgment throne,
Rock of Ages, cleft for me,
Let me hide myself in Thee!

he who had a moment before spoken of the glories of redemption passed serenely into the presence of his Redeemer. Each went his several way, leaving the bread and wine untasted. The service from which we had expected so much had been strangely interrupted. And yet all those who were present felt that it had a beauty, a sacredness, a solemnity, of its own. But for the interruption how soon that gathering would have been forgotten! Now it lives in our memories for ever! We felt as Elisha must have felt when Elijah ascended in a whirlwind before his eyes. The service was perfectly complete, after all.

For the third of these experiences I go back to my Mosgiel days. I remember being asked to speak at a farewell-meeting. The retiring minister had held the charge for over fifty years. When his turn came to speak, he made three desperate efforts to master his emotion. But it was no good. After a few broken sentences he each time collapsed; and his people felt that his silence was more eloquent than his speech could possibly have been. The best things we ever say are the things we never say.

Are there not two such occasions in the Bible—one in each Testament? 'And Moses returned unto the Lord, and said, Oh, this people have sinned a great sin, and have made them gods of gold. Yet now, if Thou wilt forgive their sin—' If—what? We shall never know what was in the old leader's mind. The prayer was interrupted; but it is all the finer for being interrupted. There are moments in which the soul leaves speech behind, as a bird leaves the bough, as a butterfly leaves its chrysalis. The New Testament instance is, of course, the story of the prodigal. 'I will arise,' he said, 'and go to my father, and will say unto him,

Father, I have sinned against heaven, and before thee, and am no more worthy to be called thy son: make me as one of thy hired servants. And he arose, and came to his father'; but the carefully prepared speech was interrupted. The last clause was never uttered. 'I am no more worthy,' he cried, 'to be called thy son——.' That was all; he said nothing about being a hired servant. The revelation of the father's love laughs out of court such squalid stipulations.

Ian Maclaren has put the same story in another setting. Flora Campbell was a prodigal daughter, and she came home. 'When she reached the door, her strength had departed and she was not able to knock. She could hear her father feeling for the latch, which for once could not be found, and saying nothing but "Flora, Flora." She had made up some kind of speech, but the only word she ever said was "Father," for Lachlan, who had never even kissed her all the days of her youth, clasped her in his arms and sobbed out blessings over her head.' Flora told Marget Howe afterwards that in the Gaelic there are fifty words for 'darling,' and that her father called her by every one of them the night she came home. And thus her carefully prepared speech was interrupted, and, like the speech of the prodigal, was immeasurably improved by the interruption.

One of the best books in the language was born of an interruption. 'I was just going to say,' it begins, 'when I was interrupted——' The interruption referred to in that opening sentence was, Dr. Oliver Wendell Holmes tells us in the introduction, just a quarter of a century in duration. But if the interruption had never occurred, and if the book had been written when it was first commenced, it is certain that *The Autocrat of the Breakfast-table* would not have been the book that we all treasure so highly and love so well.

But, like language and like literature, life itself gets sometimes interrupted, and generally comes out all the better for the interruption. Who that knows the history of Japan can ever forget the story of the Hon. Alpheus Hardy? Let him tell it in his own words. He says: 'I am not a college man, and it was the bitter disappointment of my life that I could not be one. I wanted to go to college and become a minister; so I went to Phillips Academy to fit. My health broke down, and, in spite of my determined hope of being able to go on, at last the truth was forced on me that I could not. To tell my disappointment is impossible. It seemed as if all my hope and purpose in life were defeated. "I cannot be God's minister," was the sentence that kept rolling through my mind. When that fact at last became certain to me, one morning alone in my room, my distress was so great that I threw myself flat on the floor. The voiceless cry of my soul was, "O God, I cannot be Thy minister!" Then there came to me as I lay a vision, a new hope, a perception that I could serve God in business with the same devotion as in preaching, and that to make money for God might be my sacred calling. The vision of this service, and its nature as a sacred ministry, were so clear and joyous that I rose to my feet, and, with new hope in my heart, exclaimed aloud, "O God, I *can* be Thy minister! I will go back to Boston. I will make money for God, and *that* shall be my ministry!" From that time I have felt myself as much appointed and ordained to make money for God as if I had been permitted to carry out my own plan and been ordained to preach the gospel. I am God's man, and the ministry to which God has called me is to make and administer money for Him.' He felt that his life had been interrupted, but he determined to make the interruption like the pause in the music that adds effectiveness to all that goes before it and impressiveness to all that follows after.

We all know the sequel. Alpheus Hardy came in course of time to own a line of steamers that traded with Japan. On one of them a little Japanese boy stowed away, and the captain brought him to Mr. Hardy. Mr. Hardy prayed with him, pointed him to the Saviour, and gave him a first-class University education. Then young Neesima went back to Japan to spread the Christian faith from one end of that great empire to the other, and no name in the annals of Japan is more honoured than is his. Had Alpheus Hardy had his heart's desire and been a minister, it is exceedingly problematical as to whether he could ever have wrought so fine a work as that. The interruption, like the pause of the orchestra, intensified the beauty of life's harmony.

And, coming back to the unfinished Communion Service, what is death itself but an interruption? Is it not at least conceivable that the first words that most of us will utter on the other shore will be those with which Dr. Oliver Wendell Holmes begins his book? 'I was just going to say, *when I was interrupted*——' Life, like the parts of a serial story, is always '*to be continued.*' At the close of his great history of Peter the Great, Waliszewski comments on the appropriateness of the statuary that adorns the great Czar's tomb. 'At the foot of the mausoleum,' he says, 'an ingenious inspiration has set the symbolic image of a sculptor, beside the unfinished figure his tool has chiselled in the marble.' The work was interrupted. But it is only an interruption. 'I feel,' wrote Victor Hugo, 'I feel that I have not said a thousandth part of what is in me. When I go down to the grave I shall have ended my day's work. But another day will begin next morning. Life closes in the twilight; it opens with the dawn.' As we sometimes sing:

We'll catch the broken threads again,
And finish what we here began;
Heaven will the mysteries explain,
And then, sometime, we'll understand.

And, depend upon it, when we resume our old relationships, and take up our tasks anew, we shall find that those fond friendships will have been sweetened, and those hallowed activities perfected, by the temporary break. Life as a whole will have been immeasurably enriched by the interruption.

VII

ON BEING LEFT-HANDED

A LADY friend of mine—not all the gold of the Indies would bribe me into revealing her name—is left-handed. She carves left-handed; writes left-handed; sews left-handed; indeed, her husband sometimes says that she talks left-handed. However that may be, my esteem for this lady sufficiently explains my choice of my present theme. On the face of it, there is nothing really singular about such a phenomenon. The wonder is, not that some people are left-handed, but that so many people are right-handed. Nature has done nothing towards establishing the right hand in the place of precedence. No physical law ordains that I shall put my right foot foremost. Whence, then, this slavish submission to an unwritten law? Why should we not all be left-handed? Or, at least, why should not the favours be more evenly divided? Or, better still, why should we not all be ambidextrous? Why have we left my lady friend under an embarrassing sense of singularity and isolation? Has not she at least as good a right to express a preference for her left hand as I have to thrust into special prominence my right?

Sir James Sawyer, I notice, says that the right hand gained its unnatural but commanding authority in the rude old times when all men were warriors and spent most of their time at war. 'When,' he says, 'men first fought together in companies, they must soon have found that it was most convenient to handle their weapons in a uniform way. If some in a fighting company were right-handed and others were left-handed, their weapons would be continually clashing. Whether drilling or fighting, the men would need more space for wielding their weapons. If, on the other hand, each man used his sword or his staff with the same hand as his neighbour employed, confusion would be minimized, and a symmetrical appearance would be given to the martial body.' But that does not help us very much. It only goes to show that men fighting side by side should handle their weapons with the *same* hand. It says nothing in support of the tyrannical claim of the *right* hand to absolute supremacy; it says nothing derogatory to any similar claim that the more modest left hand might be persuaded to lay. Granting all that Sir James Sawyer says, why should not all the warriors have used their left hands? Or why, at any rate, should not some of the companies have used their left hands? In very early times they certainly did, for are we not told that 'among all this people there were seven hundred chosen men left-handed; every one could sling stones at an hairbreadth and not miss'? I advise my lady friend, whenever she is invited to subscribe her signature to an autograph album, to place that quotation against her name.

I hinted in my introductory sentences that my friend's husband—we all know what husbands are—is inclined to twit his wife on her extreme left-handedness. But that kind of thing never pays in the long run. As a matter of fact, this very man had not been married many months before he discovered that there were some things that his left-handed wife could do, and do well, that he could only do very awkwardly or not at all. Indeed, even before their wedding, a hint was given him that such a revelation very possibly awaited him. With all the mingled pride and bashfulness incidental to such occasions, he one day took his bride-elect to inspect the house that was being erected for them. As they moved cautiously about the roofless and floorless skeleton of their future home, the foreman suddenly shouted for one of his men.

'Bremner! Where's Bremner?'

'He's gone over to the other job, sir,' explained one of the carpenters. 'Is it anything I can do?'

'No,' replied the foreman. 'I want a screw driven

in here, but it's an awkward corner, and only a left-handed man could get in!'

My friend smiled, and the lady beside him blushed; but very often since he has discovered that there are innumerable awkward corners that only left-handed people can skilfully negotiate.

And thus it often happens that a left-handed person and a right-handed person, like the two hands themselves, perfectly supplement each other. It often happens that the one hand is able to perform what the other hand cannot. The world is built on that plan. As each member of my body holds in charge powers that it is under obligation to exercise for the good of all the other members, and is thus a supplement to them, so each member of society holds in sacred charge gifts and graces which he is under solemn obligation to use for the general good. And just as particular members of my body are designed as supplements in a special sense to each other, so it is intended that we should supplement, and be supplemented by, those who, by circumstances or by kinship, are most nearly related to us. In his memoirs, Thomas Boston tells of the fast and fruitful friendship subsisting between Mr. Gabriel Wilson, of Maxton, and himself. This friendship, he says, 'arrived at an uncommon height and strictness. Whatever odds there was in some respects betwixt him and me, there was still a certain cast of temper by which I found him to be my other self. He was extremely modest ; but, once touched with the weight of a matter, he was very forward and keen, fearing the face of no man. On the other hand, I was slow and timorous. In the which mixture, whereby he served as a spur to me, and I as a bridle to him, I have often admired the wise conduct of Providence that matched us together.' Is not this our right-handed friend and his left-handed wife over again ?

And, after all, what on earth does it matter ? The main thing is, not to do your work in a particular way, or with a particular hand, but to do it particularly well. The seven hundred chosen men left-handed could every one sling stones at an hairbreadth and not miss. That is what counts. Their methods would doubtless be severely challenged at first. But the accuracy of their aim, and the efficiency of their service, would soon disarm all carping criticism. Towards the end of the eighteenth century, two great literary men were making valuable contributions to the enlightenment of mankind. Jean Buffon was writing his Natural History at Paris ; Samuel Johnson was editing his Dictionary in London. Buffon would only work in a room scrupulously clean and tidy, and would wash and dress, as though for a ball, before entering his study. Johnson worked in a room as dusty and untidy at can well be imagined, and the very chair on which he sat was a broken one. But the world has passed over these facts with a smile. It reads Buffon's Natural History, and it consults Johnson's Dictionary; and it pardons the idiosyncrasies of both men. Exactly a century later, history, according to her custom, repeated herself. In his library in London Macaulay bends over the manuscript of his History of England looking as though he had just returned from a dinner at Holland House. Not many streets away, Carlyle is working away at his *Frederick the Great*, so smothered with dust that 'he looks, for all the world, like a miller who had fallen into his bins one after another in the process of grinding the meal for his daily bread.' But literature welcomes both Macaulay and Carlyle.

We instinctively recall the rivalry that existed two hundred years ago between the audacious Lord Peterborough and the stolid Lord Galway. When Peterborough commanded the British armies in the field, nobody could predict his next manœuvre. He outraged all the conventions of the military schools and bewildered everybody who watched the dispositions of his troops. The only compensation was that he won all his battles and drove his enemies to despair. The Government, however, felt that it would never do to entrust the conduct of the war to so very erratic a commander. They, therefore, appointed Lord Galway in his stead. 'Galway,' says one historian, 'conducted the campaign in the most scientific manner. He drew up his troops at Almanza according to the methods prescribed by the best writers, and in a few hours lost eighteen thousand men, a hundred and twenty standards, all his baggage, and all his artillery.' Is it not better to do a thing well with the left hand than to do it badly with the right?

I suppose the feebleness and awkwardness of my left hand is one of the most forceful illustrations I could have of the penalty attendant upon neglect. Why is my left hand weaker than my right? Is it because it was made so, or intended to be so? Of course not; it is because it has been neglected, and has never received the attention that has been lavished upon its companion. Henry Drummond and Charles Darwin have said all that needs to be said on that subject. I lived for some years in New Zealand. In New Zealand you will find 'wingless birds.' But a 'wingless bird' is a contradiction in terms. A bird, in its very nature, must have wings. And these birds had. But, finding it more pleasant to hop about the earth than to soar into the air, their neglect of their pinions soon led to their forfeiting them altogether. And when, later on, the country was invaded by stoats and weasels, the miserable creatures, unable now to fly, fell an easy prey to the enemies they might otherwise have despised.

But this left-handed lady of mine reminds me of a

happier law—the law of compensation. I find that most people who are left-handed owe it to some early injury inflicted upon the right hand. The one hand became temporarily disabled; the other took its place; and the original worker was never reinstated. On the disablement of the one, the other swiftly became as quick, as sensitive, and as useful as the other had been. It has often been remarked that a person deprived of one faculty soon develops other powers almost to the point of adequate compensation. Now, there are many people who have been bitterly disappointed in life. It is as though they have been deprived of the use of their right hand. The temptation is to give up. My right hand is injured, what can I do? But left-handed people point us to a quite opposite conclusion. If you are denied your right hand, make the most of your left. If one of our greatest sailors and one of our greatest soldiers had not argued on these lines, two of our greatest British battles would never have been won. Nelson lost his right arm at Santa Cruz. He might have said, 'I have no right arm, and I have lost an eye; I will give it up!' Then we should have had no Trafalgar! The doctors shook their heads gravely over Wolfe when a boy, and said that he could not possibly live long. Wolfe might have decided that there was nothing for it but to sit and mope away his few years in melancholy indolence. But he argued the other way. He resolved to make the very most of what years were destined to be his. He enlisted, and earned rapid promotion. He was a general before he was thirty. And, in his thirty-second year, to the amazement of mankind, he took Quebec. He fell in the hour of his magnificent triumph, having lived as brilliantly, and dying as gloriously, as he could possibly have wished.

I see that one of our authorities, in accounting for the prevalence of right-handed fighting, suggests that, when men came to use swords in their warfare, and to fight hand to hand, it became necessary, above all things, to keep the heart as far from the antagonist as possible. To fight with the left hand would have exposed that vital organ ; to fight with the right hand would protect it. There is a wealth of philosophy just there. 'Keep the heart with all diligence,' said one of the wisest of men, 'for out of it are the issues of life.' We recall the old story of the conversation between Sir Walter Raleigh and his executioner. It is said that the executioner told his noble victim that he would find the scaffold more comfortable if he turned his head the other way Whereupon Sir Walter replied, 'My friend, it matters little how the *head* lies so long as the *heart* is right!' We cannot do better than leave the matter there.

VIII

'HOME, SWEET HOME!'

STROLLING through the bush on Tuesday afternoon with a couple of companions, we came suddenly and unexpectedly in sight of the sea. Fifty yards away to the left, on the crest of the ridge, lay a great log. Nobody suggested a rest; but it seemed the natural thing to do. We were all three a little hot and tired after our climb; and, as though by instinct, we broke into the scrub, and were soon sitting together on the fallen tree. It was a bright day, with a clear blue sky, and the sea was a sheet of sapphire. There, on the summit of Blue Spur, we sat in silence for a minute or two. And then.

'Do you know what this reminds me of?' asked one of my companions.

'Well,' he went on, in response to our inevitably negative replies, 'it reminds me of the first days that I spent in Australia. Talk about being homesick! Why, I used to think of England all day and dream of England all night. The process of awaking every morning represented a rude snatching of my soul from a sweet English fancy to a stern Australian fact. On opening my eyes, I always looked round me in uttermost bewilderment, wondering where on earth I was. And on Sunday afternoons I used to climb to the top of a hill very much like this, look out across the sea, and cry like a baby.'

We all understood, for, years ago, we had all three made the same great venture. No man ever yet left the Homeland behind him, and settled under these southern stars, without passing through some such agonizing experience.

I

Homesickness is the only kind of sickness from which the world has very greatly benefited. But we have made enough profit on homesickness to wipe off the deficit on all the other maladies put together. One of these days this old world of ours will suddenly come to recognize how much it owes to its own homesickness. I have just been reading the *Life* of Professor Morse, the inventor of telegraphy. What put such a daring notion into his head? He was an artist, not an engineer! How did it come to pass that this struggling young American painter, starving in Europe, should confer upon mankind so inestimable a boon? The story is easily told. He was homesick; that was all. He wanted to speak to his mother, and to speak at once.

He had crossed the ocean; and only the emigrant knows what a pitiless thing the ocean seems to be as the chasm widens between himself and everything he loves. In the course of a tedious voyage, that occupied nearly a month, Samuel Morse crossed the Atlantic. As he approached the shores of Europe he reflected that nearly three months would have passed from the time of his sorrowful farewell to his parents to the time of the arrival of his first letter from abroad. Three months! 'I only wish,' he says in that first letter, 'I only wish you had this letter now to relieve your minds from anxiety, for while I am writing I can imagine mother wishing that she could hear of my arrival, and thinking of thousands of accidents which may have befallen me. I wish that in an instant I could communicate the information. But three thousand miles are not passed over in an instant.' And yet why should they not be? That was the question that the homesick young artist revolved within his troubled brain. And he worried away at it until at last he taught the world the mysteries of telegraphy.

II

No, my companion of Tuesday afternoon was not the first Australian to experience the pangs of home-sickness. The first settlers knew just such tempests of ungovernable emotion. I have talked with some of the first white men who ever landed in New Zealand, and they have told me just such tales as my friend confided to me as we sat chatting on the crest of the Blue Spur. Many a hardy pathfinder left the quiet and tranquil village sleeping in the drowsy sunshine of an English June; he said a sad good-bye to the meadows all ablaze with buttercups, to the lanes all fragrant with hawthorn, to the old grey church, to the pretty village green, to the dreamy inn, the gabled cottage, and the rose-covered porch; he crossed the interminable leagues of salt, estranging sea, and plunged into the vast Australian solitudes. The change from the dear familiar fields that he had left to the wilderness of tussock and the tangle of bush to which he had come was a violent one; and the stoutest-hearted pioneer knew what it was to look back across the sea with dim eyes and thoughts too deep for utterance. But, like brave men, they cured their home-sickness by resolving to establish in these new lands a home life that would be as dear to their children as their own had been to them. And so, with aching hearts, but with firm and steady hands, they laid, well and truly, the foundations of a new nation. They built the first Australian farms, the first Australian churches, the first Australian schools, and the first Australian homes.

III

Yes, the first Australian churches. For it is wonderful how large a place the old grey church occupies in our homesick dreams. How, when we first arrived, it all rushed back upon the memory, sweeping us off our feet in an uncontrollable gust of emotion! The leisurely walk across the fields to the music of the bells; the friendly greetings by the gate; the cheery handshake in the porch; the flutter of children in their Sunday dresses; the restful stillness of the quiet old building; and the little peculiarities attaching to the individualities of the worshippers. It all seemed so humdrum and commonplace in the old days; but as a memory from afar it was the concentration of enchantment. It was only when all the waves of the world rolled between us and it that we discovered how dear it all was to us; and the only mitigation of our anguish lay in the attempt to reproduce on this side of the world the choicest things that we had left behind us.

IV

I am afraid to speak of heaven, for the very mention of such a theme presents two difficulties. There is the difficulty of those who think that we ought to be homesick *for* heaven, and there is the difficulty of those who fancy that we may be homesick *in* heaven. Dr. Oliver Wendell Holmes has a striking little poem expressing this idea. 'Most people,' he says, 'love this world more than they are willing to confess, and it is hard to conceive ourselves weaned from it so as to feel no emotion at the thought of its most sacred recollections—even after a sojourn of years, as we should count the lapse of earthly time—in the realm where, sooner or later, all tears shall be wiped away.' In the poem he pictures the homesick inhabitants of heaven thinking wistfully of the earth they have left:

> For there we loved, and where we love is home,
>   Home that our feet may leave, but not our hearts,
> Though o'er us shine the jasper-lighted dome:—
>   The chain may lengthen, but it never parts!
>
> Sometimes a sunlit sphere comes rolling by,
>   And then we softly whisper—can it be?
> And leaning toward the silvery orb, we try
>   To hear the music of its murmuring sea;
>
> To catch, perchance, some flashing glimpse of green,
>   Or breathe some wild-wood fragrance, wafted through
> The opening gates of pearl, that fold between
>   The blinding splendours and the changeless blue

He pictures a woman, caught away in the hour of childbirth, crying to go back to her motherless babe; a bride, snatched away when her felicity was at its height, longing to return to her disconsolate bridegroom; whilst a third protests that her cravings for earth are prompted by no such emotions.

Nay, tax not me with passion's wasting fire;
When the swift message set my spirit free,
Blind, helpless, lone, I left my grey-haired sire;
My friends were many; he had none save me.

I left him, orphaned, in the starless night;
Alas, for him no cheerful morning's dawn!
I wear the ransomed spirit's robe of white,
Yet still I hear him moaning, She is gone!

These fancies only go to show what grotesque caricatures our thoughts of heaven really are. All that we know about heaven we know from Scripture. But, if Scripture is more clear about one thing than about another, it is this: that heaven will perfectly satisfy all who reach it. It follows that any idea of heaven that assumes some of its inhabitants to be unhappy is false to fact. The trouble is, as Mr. H. G. Wells would say, that you cannot describe the life of one world in the language of another. Our fears of discontent arise from our ignorance of the things beyond our ken. In heaven, we are told, there shall be no manner of sickness—not even homesickness. Heaven will be wondrously homely. Heaven will be home.

V

At the opposite pole there are those who are troubled because, although they think of heaven as home, they are conscious of no homesickness concerning it. They are in no hurry to die. The hymns expressive of a passionate longing for heaven do not fit their mood at all. I advise these good people not to worry. It is only a question of time. Life is built on sane principles. Our appetites only become keen as the hour approaches for their gratification. It is towards dinner-time that we begin to feel desperately hungry. It is towards evening that we begin to long for rest. Most old people, however fully they may have entered into the zest and enjoyment of life, feel that they have had just about enough of it. They grow gradually out of love with the things that are, and fall in love with the things that are to be. 'Some of us have but few years to live,' said Dr. Dale, when nearing the end. 'The evening star is in the darkening sky. The autumn leaves are falling around us. We seem to be walking through fields of stubble, from which the poor harvests of our past toil have been already gathered.' The right feeling comes at the right time. Homesickness overtakes us when our steps are homeward bent.

VI

And is there not a homesickness that only the soul knows? By what touch of spiritual genius does the story of the Prodigal Son find a place in the New Testament? An American writer has recently reminded us that 'it is not argument and persuasion that most often sends the prodigal on his way back to the fatted calf and the robe and the ring of civilized life. It is much more frequently the haphazard vision of a stranger's lamp-lit hall, or the glow of a kitchen fire seen through an area railing. It is such things that awaken the unbearable homesickness, and suddenly render the swine and the husks detestable. In the far country there came to the prodigal, not a brilliant oration or a powerful argument, but an overwhelming rush of memory. He saw once more the dear old home that had sheltered his earliest infancy; he looked in fancy into the drawn and wistful face of his waiting father; he thought he beheld once more the familiar forms of the hired servants as they went their accustomed rounds. It all swept over him with extraordinary fascination and fondness. It was too much for him. Homesickness poured into his soul like the ocean streaming through broken dikes.' 'I will arise and go!' he exclaimed. And, depend upon it, this poor ministry of mine will be most fruitful when

I can awaken in men such an agony of homesickness that their hearts will cry out for the Father. In some witching little verses Miss Susie M. Best makes a dead man say:

> When I was laid in my coffin,
> Quite done with Time and its fears,
> My son came and stood beside me—
> He hadn't been home for years;
> And right on my face came dripping
> The scald of his salty tears;
> And I was so glad to know his breast
> Had turned at last to the old home nest,
> That I said to myself (in an underbreath):
> 'This is the recompense of death.'

It is an allegory. The joy that made the Cross despicable to the Crucified was the joy of knowing that its anguish would turn the hearts of His prodigals towards Home.